RECIPES

A COLLEGE STUDENT'S COOKBOOK

By: Bradley G. Hamilton

Spruce Street Publishing

Published in 1999 by
Spruce Street Publishing
35D Spruce Street
Toronto, Ontario
M5A 2H8
(416) 922-6017

Canadian Cataloguing in Publication Data

Hamilton, Bradley Gavin, 1964-
Recipes 'A' Rez: A College Student's Cookbook

ISBN   0-9684366-1-7

        1.Quick and easy cookery   2.Low budget cookery
TX652.H345 1999   641.5'12   C99-900123-X

Design by Brett Feschuk for Amoeba Corp.
Illustrations by Jason Edmiston.

Printed and bound in Canada.

To my best friend in
the world, my mom. Thanks
for all the great recipes,
without them, I would have
never made it through my
college days.

love Brad

Yo, College Kids,

Are you tired of canned soup, spaghetti, and cafeteria delights? If you aren't yet you soon will be--that's why I took all my Mom's recipes that she sent me off to College with and put them in this survival cookbook for you...I've been there, done that, got the t-shirt.

Recipes "И" Rez is a cookbook for College kids full of my Mom's delicious recipes. They got me through College and they will get you through it too. It doesn't matter if you're grabbing a quick bite on the run or making that special dinner for that special someone... this cookbook has it all.

So, enjoy the College Cuisine you will soon be making as you study to pass the course of College Cooking 101 with the help of Recipes "И" Rez!

Enjoy!

SECTIONS

SOUPS, SALADS, & SANDWICHES

DIET DELIGHT SOUP

1	can cream of chicken soup
1/4	cup juice from canned mushrooms
1	cup non-fat milk (skim)
1/2	cup water
1/2	tsp. curry powder
1	tbsp. chopped green onions
2	cups favourite vegetables

Combine all ingredients, heat slowly over medium heat. Stir until smooth. Serve.

SOUTH OF THE BORDER SOUP

2	pounds fresh tomatoes
1	whole cucumber (peeled and seeded)
1	large onion (diced)
1	clove garlic
1	red bell pepper
1/2	pound of white bread crumbs (soaked in water)
1/2	cup olive oil
1/2	cup vinegar

salt and pepper to taste

Combine all ingredients in blender and puree. Chill overnight. Add water to thin to desired consistency.

MYSTERY MEAT SOUP

1/2	pound lean ground beef
1	medium onion
1	28 ounce can of tomatoes
2	cups water
3	cans consomme soup
1	can tomato soup
4	carrots (diced)
3	sticks celery (diced)
1	bay leaf
1/2	tsp. thyme
8	tbsp. barley
1	tbsp. parsley

Brown meat and onions, drain well and add to other ingredients in a large pot. Simmer covered, and cook for at least 2 to 3 hours on medium heat. Serve.

MOTTO MINESTRONE SOUP

1	16 ounce can red kidney beans
6	cups chicken stock
1/2	cup uncooked rice
1/4	pound bacon
2	stalks celery (chopped)
2	cups each of spinach, cabbage, and carrots (chopped)
1	cup raw turnips (diced)
1	cup canned diced tomatoes
1	medium onion (diced)
1/2	cup fresh parsley (minced)
1	clove garlic (minced)
1/3	cup parmesan cheese
	pinch of powdered sage
	salt and pepper to taste

In a large kettle bring stock to the boiling point. Add the kidney beans and all remaining ingredients except cheese. Reduce heat to simmer and cook until vegetables are tender. Top with parmesan cheese and season with salt and pepper when serving.

Ivy League Soup

8	cups water
1	tbsp. butter
2	cups frozen peas
1	cup carrots (diced)
2	cups shredded cabbage
1/2	cup fresh parsley (minced)
1	cup heavy cream
1	tsp. salt

Put water and salt into pot. Bring to boil. Add peas and carrots. Cook until partly tender. Add cabbage and parsley. Cook on low heat until tender. Add butter and cream. Stir and serve piping hot.

CAMBRIDGE CLAM CHOWDER SOUP

2   cups potatoes (diced)

4   slices bacon (chopped)

2   tbsp. butter

1/4 cup flour

1   cup onion (chopped)

1/2 tsp. salt

1/4 tsp. pepper

2   cans clams and juice

3   cups milk or cream

dash of Worcestershire sauce

dash of nutmeg

Partly boil potatoes (approx. 10 minutes). Fry bacon until crisp, then add butter and sauté onions until translucent. Add flour, salt and pepper, stir until smooth. Cook for 3 minutes. Stir in clam juice, cream and potatoes. Add nutmeg, Worcestershire sauce and clams. Simmer until potatoes are tender. Serve.

"Parlez Vous" Onion Soup

4 medium onions (chopped)
2 tbsp. butter
6 slices bacon
2 cups water
3 bouillon beef cubes
4 slices Gruyere cheese
2 eggs (beaten)
2 cups milk
salt and pepper to taste

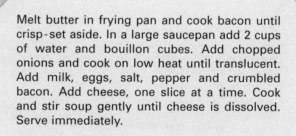

Melt butter in frying pan and cook bacon until crisp-set aside. In a large saucepan add 2 cups of water and bouillon cubes. Add chopped onions and cook on low heat until translucent. Add milk, eggs, salt, pepper and crumbled bacon. Add cheese, one slice at a time. Cook and stir soup gently until cheese is dissolved. Serve immediately.

POTATOE "QUAYLE" SOUP

4   medium potatoes (diced)
3   carrots (sliced)
2   tbsp. chopped onion
6   cups water
3   strips bacon (crumbled)
2   tbsp. flour
1/4 tsp. parsley
salt and pepper to taste

Combine above ingredients, except bacon and flour, in a large pot and cook until vegetables are tender. In a pan, sauté the bacon until crisp. Add the flour to the bacon and brown, then add some of the broth from the pot to make a sauce. Add this back to the large pot and stir well. Bring back to the boil, then simmer. Serve.

Tommy Toe Soup

1 can cream of tomato soup
2 cups milk
1/4 tsp. garlic powder
1/4 tsp. paprika
1/2 cup cream cheese (cubed)
1 small onion (chopped)
2 tbsp. butter
1/4 tsp. salt

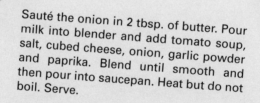

Sauté the onion in 2 tbsp. of butter. Pour milk into blender and add tomato soup, salt, cubed cheese, onion, garlic powder and paprika. Blend until smooth and then pour into saucepan. Heat but do not boil. Serve.

MIGHTY MUSHROOM SOUP

3 1/2	cups milk
3	cups mushrooms (sliced)
1/4	cup white onion (finely chopped)
1/4	cup plain yogurt
1/4	cup sour cream
1/3	cup flour
1/4	cup milk
1/4	cup butter
3	chicken bouillon cubes
1/2	tsp. soya sauce
1/2	tsp. thyme
1/2	tsp. parsley

salt and pepper to taste

Place mushrooms, onion and butter in large pan and cook over medium heat until tender. Combine milk and flour and blend into paste. Add chicken bouillon cubes, thyme, soya sauce, and parsley. Stir continuously until sauce thickens. Just prior to serving, add yogurt and sour cream and mix well. Serve immediately.

SUPER SIMPLE SALAD

1 1/2   cups chicken (cooked and diced)
1   cup apples (diced)
3/4   cup celery (diced)
1   tbsp. sweet pickles (chopped)
1/2   cup mayonnaise

Mix together above ingredients (to taste). Serve on lettuce leaves. Garnish with pineapple slices, carrot sticks, tomato quarters and/or olives.

SORORITY SALAD

1   cup pineapple tidbits
1   tin mandarin oranges
1   tin apricots (chopped)
2   egg yolks
2   pkgs. lemon Jell-o
1/2 cup whipped cream

Drain fruit and reserve juice. Combine all fruit juices in top of a double boiler with 2 beaten egg yolks. Cook until it forms a thin custard. Stir in 2 pkgs. of lemon Jell-O. Chill until it starts to thicken. Fold in fruit and add 1/2 cup of whipped cream. Keep chilled until ready to serve. If you want to get really fancy pour the mixture into a large mold to set.

BREAKFAST SALAD

1	medium head of lettuce
3	hard cooked eggs (chopped)
1/4	pound bacon (cooked and crumbled)
1-2	green onions (chopped)
2	tbsp. vinegar
1	tsp. Worcestershire sauce

freshly ground pepper

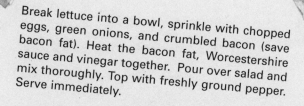

Break lettuce into a bowl, sprinkle with chopped eggs, green onions, and crumbled bacon (save bacon fat). Heat the bacon fat, Worcestershire sauce and vinegar together. Pour over salad and mix thoroughly. Top with freshly ground pepper. Serve immediately.

CABARET COLESLAW

1   small green or red cabbage
    (finely chopped)
1   tbsp. butter
1   tbsp. flour
1   tsp. sugar
1   tsp. salt
1   tsp. dry mustard
2   eggs (beaten)
1/2 pint light cream
2   tbsp. vinegar
dash of pepper

Cream butter with flour, sugar, salt, dry mustard and a dash of pepper. Add beaten eggs. Mix well. Add light cream. Heat vinegar, add to first mixture and cook until thick. Cool and add to finely chopped cabbage. About 1/2 cup of dressing for every 2 cups of cabbage. Serve chilled.

"Seizure" Salad

2	large heads of romaine lettuce
2	cups croutons
1/4	cup olive oil
2	cloves of garlic
1	egg
1/2	tsp. salt
1	lemon
1/2	cup grated parmesan cheese
2 - 3	anchovy fillets (optional)
	freshly ground black pepper

Rub the bottom of a large salad bowl with the garlic cloves then mince. Tear lettuce into pieces, wash and pat dry. Blend all ingredients until smooth. Pour over lettuce. Add cheese and anchovies. Mix well. Top with croutons before serving.

LOUISIANA CHICKEN GUMBO SALAD

1   can chicken gumbo soup
1   can flaked tuna
1/2   cup celery (finely diced)
1/4   cup onion (chopped)
1   pkg. lemon Jell-O
1/2   cup boiling water
1/2   cup mayonnaise
1/2   cup whipped cream

Dissolve Jell-O in hot water and add the can of soup. When cool, add celery, onion and tuna. Fold in mayonnaise and whipped cream. Chill until ready to serve.
Diced green peppers and pimento may be added for flavour and colour.

Graduation Greens Salad

Salad:

2   pkgs. fresh spinach
1/2 pkg. seasoned stuffing mix
3   hard boiled eggs (diced)
1/4 pound bacon (fried and crumbled)

Dressing:

1/3 cup oil
1/3 cup vinegar
3   tsp. prepared mustard
2/3 cup sugar
1   tsp. celery seed
1   tsp. salt
1/2 tsp. pepper

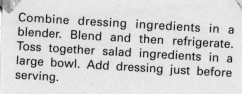

Combine dressing ingredients in a blender. Blend and then refrigerate. Toss together salad ingredients in a large bowl. Add dressing just before serving.

Party Potato Salad

10 - 12	medium potatoes (4 pounds)
6	slices bacon (cooked and crumbled)
1	cup celery (diced)
2	tbsp. onion (finely chopped)
4	tsp. salt
1/2	cup butter
1/4	cup flour
1/2	tsp. dry mustard
3	tbsp. sugar
1	cup beer
1	tsp. tabasco
2	tbsp. parsley (chopped)

Boil potatoes, peel and dice. Add bacon, celery and onion. Sprinkle with 2 tsp. of salt. Melt butter in small sauce pan and add flour, mustard, sugar and remaining 2 tsp. of salt. Stir over low heat until it forms a smooth paste. Gradually add the beer and cook, stirring constantly until the mixture comes to a boil (starts to thicken). Add tabasco and pour mixture over potatoes, sprinkle with parsley. Mix together lightly. Let stand for 1 hour. Cover and reheat in a 375 degree oven for 25 minutes. For the mega party!!

HIGH THAI SALAD

1	pound round steak (sliced in thin strips)
3/4	cup catalina salad dressing
1	cup mushrooms (sliced)
1	small head of lettuce (shredded)
1/4	cup bean sprouts
3	tbsp. crushed peanuts
3	tbsp. soya sauce
1	tbsp. brown sugar
2	tbsp. fresh coriander
2	tsp. red pepper flakes

Place steak strips in bowl and marinate in salad dressing for a minimum of 4 hours. Broil steak strips until cooked, then set aside. Heat the remaining marinade in a saucepan, add soya sauce, brown sugar, red pepper flakes and mushrooms. Add the steak strips to reheat. Place shredded lettuce on plate, place beef strips over top and cover with bean sprouts, peanuts and coriander. Serve warm.

ITCHI- BITCHY SALAD

Salad:

3	cups bean sprouts
2	cups mushrooms (sliced)
1/2	head of cabbage (shredded)
1/2	cup sliced almonds (toasted)
1/4	cup green onions (chopped)
1/4	cup unsalted sunflower seeds
2	tbsp. sesame seeds
1	pkg. Ichiban noodle soup (crushed)

Dressing:

1/2	cup oil
3	tbsp. vinegar
2	tbsp. soya sauce
1	tbsp. sugar
1	pkg. seasoning mix from soup

salt and pepper to taste

Place all dressing ingredients in a glass jar and shake until well mixed. In a large bowl, toss cabbage, bean sprouts, green onions, mushrooms, sunflower seeds, almonds, and crushed noodles. Pour dressing over and mix well. Serve immediately.

SEASIDE SANDWICH

2   cups crab meat or tuna
3   large green onions (chopped)
3   tbsp. lemon juice
1/4 cup ketchup
5   tbsp. mayonnaise
2   eggs (separated)
1/3 cup cheese (shredded)
8   slices toast

Combine crab or tuna, onions, lemon juice, ketchup, and 1 tbsp. of mayonnaise. Mix with fork and spread on toast. In another bowl, blend remaining 4 tbsp. of mayonnaise, dash of lemon juice, egg yolks and cheese. Beat egg whites until they form firm peaks and fold into mayonnaise mixture. Spread over sandwiches and broil in oven for 3-4 minutes until just golden. Absolutely Fabulous!

Greek Week Wiener Sandwich

4	wieners (chopped)
1 1/2	cups bread crumbs
1/4	cup milk
1/3	cup melted butter
6	eggs
1/2	cup cheese (grated)

salt and pepper to taste

Combine wieners, bread crumbs, milk and butter. Place mixture in a muffin tin. Hollow out and place an egg in the middle of each. Sprinkle with cheese and salt and pepper. Bake at 150 degrees for 20 minutes.

FLAT HAT CLUB SANDWICH

2   eggs (hard boiled)
2   tbsp. mayonnaise
1/2   tsp. mustard
1   tsp. pimento (chopped)
1/2   tsp. green onions (chopped)
salt and pepper to taste

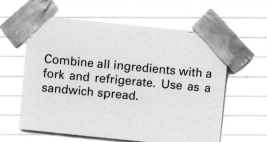

Combine all ingredients with a fork and refrigerate. Use as a sandwich spread.

SPANKIN' THE SPAM SANDWICH

1 can luncheon meat (Spam)
1/4 cup sweet pickle relish
1/4 cup celery (finely chopped)
1 tsp. prepared mustard
2-3 tbsp. mayonnaise
whole wheat bread

Mash luncheon meat with a fork. Blend in relish, celery, mustard and enough mayonnaise to moisten. Spread filling on bread and garnish as desired.

Sigma Sandwich

1	pound hamburger
1/4	cup green onions (chopped)
2	tbsp. butter (melted)
1	tin mushroom soup
1/2	tsp. salt
2	tbsp. flour
1	cup sour cream

Brown hamburger and combine with all other ingredients. Spread on an open bun and warm in oven for 10-12 minutes at 325 degrees.

HOLY HOSER
SANDWICH, EH!

4	kaiser buns (sliced in half)
8	slices Canadian or peameal bacon (fried)
4	slices canned pineapple rings
4	green pepper rings
4	slices Swiss cheese

mayonnaise

dried parsley

garlic salt

Spread each kaiser slice with mayonnaise and a dash of garlic salt. Top with pineapple ring, green pepper rings, cheese and 2 slices of Canadian bacon. Broil sandwiches for 4 minutes. Garnish with parsley.

MONTE CRISTO SANDWICH

4   slices cooked ham
4   slices chicken
4   slices Swiss cheese
1/2 cup milk
3   eggs (beaten)
1/2 tsp. salt
8   slices of white bread

Combine milk, eggs and salt together. Layer ham, chicken and cheese between 2 bread slices. Dip sandwich into the egg and milk mixture and fry in butter until both sides are golden brown.

SANTORINI GYRO-WICH

3   pita bread pockets
1/2   pound roast beef (sliced)
1   cup avocado (sliced)
1   cup lettuce (shredded)
3/4   cup mayonnaise
1/4   cup milk
1/4   cup red onion (diced)
1/4   cup feta cheese
1/4   cup sliced black olives (optional)
1/4   tsp. paprika
1/4   tsp. oregano
1   small tomato (diced)
salt and pepper to taste

Mix mayonnaise, milk, oregano, paprika, salt and pepper together. Cut pita pockets in half and spread mixture on both sides of pocket. Stuff pocket with beef, avocado, lettuce, onion, tomato, olives and cheese. If desired, top with more sauce. Serve.

TOTALLY TUNA SANDWICH

1	small can tuna in water (drained and flaked)
1	cup plain yogurt
1/2	cup lettuce
1/2	cup cucumber (diced)
1/4	cup celery (sliced)
2	tbsp. sweet pickles (chopped)
1	tbsp. flour
1	tbsp. margarine
1	tsp. garlic salt
1/2	tsp. onion powder

cheese slices

Melt margarine in a medium size saucepan. Add onion powder, garlic salt, and flour. Stir until pasty, add yogurt and cook over low heat until sauce thickens. Add celery, pickles, tuna. Stir together and remove from heat. On a slice of bread or a pita pocket, assemble lettuce, cucumber and approximately 1/2 cup of tuna mixture. Cover with slice of cheese and broil for 2-3 minutes. Serve.

AWESOME ASPARAGUS SANDWICH

3	cups milk
1 1/2	cups cheese whiz
2	tbsp. margarine
1	tbsp. flour
1	can asparagus (stems+pieces, drained)
1	hard boiled egg (diced)

salt and pepper

In a medium size saucepan, melt margarine. Stir in flour and blend until pasty. Add milk and cheese and cook over medium to high heat stirring constantly. Once sauce thickens, add asparagus and egg. Mix well and add salt and pepper. Toast bread and spoon mixture over it. Serve.

MY FAVORITE "SSS" RECIPES

UP CHUCK STEW

Stew:

2   pounds beef chuck stew meat
1   pkg. onion soup mix
1   can mushroom soup
1   can mushrooms (stems and pieces)
1   cup water

Dumplings:

2   cups flour
1   cup milk
4   tsp. baking powder
1   tsp. salt
2   tbsp. butter

Mix all ingredients for the stew together and put into covered casserole dish. Bake at 325 degrees for 3 hours.

Mix all dry ingredients for dumplings with butter using a fork. Add milk until it forms a sticky dough. Place spoonfuls on top of stew and bake for an additional 15 minutes.

HANGOVER HELPER

1/2 cup uncooked rice
4   medium sliced potatoes
1   medium sliced onion
3 - 4 sliced carrots
1   pound ground beef (raw)
1/2 cup grated cheddar cheese
1   can stewed tomatoes
bread crumbs

Grease a large casserole dish and place all of the above ingredients inside in layers. Top with bread crumbs. Cover casserole and bake for 30 minutes at 400 degrees. Remove lid and cook for an additional 1 1/2 hours at 375 degrees.

If this doesn't stop the stomach ache....nothing will!!

I'RISH PUB PORK CASSEROLE

1	pound pork sausage
1/4	cup green pepper (chopped)
2	cups raw vegetables (your choice)
1	medium onion (chopped)
1	cup tomato sauce
1/2	cup shredded cheese

Brown sausages in frying pan until cooked. Put into casserole dish with other ingredients and cook covered at 400 degrees for 30 minutes. Top with crushed potato chips and serve.

What is Irish about this dish.....
nothing, I'rish I had it more often.

Campus Cabbage Rolls

1/2 pound ground beef
12 large cabbage leaves (cooked)
1 cup rice (cooked)
1 onion (chopped)
4 tbsp. tomato paste
1-2 cups tomato juice
1 beef bouillon cube
1/4 tsp. sage
1/4 tsp. garlic salt
1/4 tsp. thyme
1/4 tsp. basil
salt and pepper to taste

Boil cabbage leaves until tender. Mix all other ingredients together. Place a large scoop of the filling on a cabbage leaf and roll up securely. Repeat until all of the mixture has been used. Place cabbage rolls in a large casserole dish lined with cabbage leaves. Cover with tomato juice, add beef bouillon cube and top with a few chunks of butter. Bake 1 hour at 350 degrees.

CHILI WILLIE CHOW

1 1/2	pounds ground beef
1	large onion (diced)
1	large green pepper (chopped)
3	stalks celery (chopped)
1	can diced tomatoes
1	can tomato soup
1	can kidney beans
2	tbsp. chili powder
1	tbsp. Worcestershire sauce

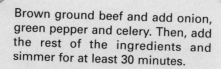

Brown ground beef and add onion, green pepper and celery. Then, add the rest of the ingredients and simmer for at least 30 minutes.

MACHO MEN DO EAT QUICHE

1   baked pastry shell
1   cup ham (cubed)
1   pound spinach (cooked and drained)
4   eggs (beaten)
1   cup heavy cream
3/4 cup bread crumbs
1   tbsp. melted butter
2   tbsp. cheese (grated)

Place ham in bottom of pie shell. Combine spinach with eggs, cream and bread crumbs and pour over ham. Sprinkle top with grated cheese and butter. Bake at 450 degrees for 20 minutes.

HOME COMING CASSEROLE

2	cups chicken (cooked and cubed)
1	cup celery (chopped)
1	cup slivered almonds (optional)
2	cups cooked rice
1	cup mayonnaise
1	can cream of chicken soup
1	can cream of mushroom soup
2	tbsp. chopped onion
2	tbsp. lemon juice
2	chicken bouillon cubes (dissolved)

salt and pepper to taste

Combine all ingredients, mixing thoroughly. Place in casserole dish and bake uncovered at 400 degrees for 45 minutes.

BOYFRIEND'S CASSEROLE

3   cups turkey (cooked and diced)
2   hard cooked eggs (chopped)
1   can sliced mushrooms
3/4 cup celery (chopped)
1/2 cup almonds
1   tbsp. grated onion
1   can cream of chicken soup
1   can chow mein noodles

Combine all ingredients in a casserole dish. Sprinkle noodles on top and bake at 350 degrees for 30 minutes.

He can be such a turkey!!

MAMA'S SOUTHERN FRIED CHICKEN

2	pounds of chicken pieces
1	cup milk
1/2	tsp. salt
1/4	tsp. pepper
1/4	tsp. paprika
1	large onion (chopped)
2	green onions
1/4	cup cooking oil
1/2	tsp. basil
1/2	tsp. parsley
1	cup flour

Soak chicken for 2 hours in milk, onion, and seasonings. Drain chicken and roll in flour. Heat oil in frying pan and add chicken. Fry over medium heat and turn (5 minutes a side). Reduce temperature and cover. Cook for an additional 20 minutes, turning occasionally until golden brown.

To make a milk gravy, add 2 tbsp. of flour to the pan drippings and stir over high heat until flour is a golden brown. Add one cup of milk in which the chicken soaked. Continue cooking, stirring until thick.

"Everything but the Kitchen Sink" Casserole

1 1/2   pounds hamburger
1   large onion (diced)
1   green pepper (chopped)
1   cup celery (chopped)
1 1/   cups stewed tomatoes
1   small can tomato sauce
2   tbsp. cooking oil
1   cup minute rice
1   can mushrooms

Fry hamburger, onion, green pepper, and celery until the meat is browned. Drain excess fat and add remaining ingredients. Mix together and put in a covered casserole dish. Bake for 1 hour at 350 degrees.

O'LA MEXICAN CHICKEN CASSEROLE

4   large boneless chicken breasts
1   can cream of mushroom soup
1/2   medium onion (chopped)
1   small can of green chilies
1   small can stewed tomatoes
1   small pkg. corn chips
3/4   cup grated cheddar cheese

Combine onion, tomatoes, chilies and soup and simmer for 1/2 hour. Spread corn chips in the bottom of a large flat baking dish. Place in chicken breasts and pour in sauce. Top with cheese. Bake uncovered for 40 minutes at 350 degrees. Serves four.

"OH NO, MY TURN TO COOK" CASSEROLE

2	cups cooked rice
3	cups cooked chicken (diced)
1	can cream of chicken soup
1	can cream of mushroom soup
1	cup mushrooms
1	cup water
1	tsp. curry powder
1/2	tsp. chili powder
1/2	cup frozen peas
4	slices bacon (fried crisp, crumbled)
1/2	cup celery
1/4	cup onion
1/2	cup green pepper

Sauté onion, celery and green pepper in cooking oil until soft and then combine with all remaining ingredients in large casserole dish. Bake for 1 hour at 350 degrees. Serve.

SPANISH NITES DELIGHT

1	pkg. flat egg noodles (cooked)
2	gloves garlic
1	large chopped onion
1	medium chopped green pepper
1 1/2	pounds ground beef
1	tbsp. Worcestershire sauce
2	cans tomato soup
1	can whole corn kernels
1	can button mushrooms
1/4	tsp. paprika

salt and pepper to taste

Cook ground beef until brown, drain off fat. Add drained noodles. Mix all above ingredients and bake in a casserole dish for 1 hour in a slow cooking oven at a temperature of 200 degrees.

TUNA TIME
EXPRESS CASSEROLE

1	can cream of mushroom soup
1	cup milk
3	cups medium size egg noodles
1	cup frozen peas
1	can tuna (water), drained and flaked
1/4	cup sliced pimiento-stuffed olives (optional)
1/2	cup grated parmesan cheese

Combine soup and milk in a saucepan. Place over medium heat and bring to a boil, stirring until blended. Add noodles. Cover and reduce heat to low. Simmer, stirring often until noodles are cooked. Remove from heat. Stir in tuna and olives. Turn all ingredients into a casserole dish, sprinkle top with parmesan cheese. Place in oven under broiler for 2 to 3 minutes or until golden brown. Serve.

PERFECT POTATO CASSEROLE

2	pounds frozen hash brown potatoes
2	cups sour cream
2	cans cream of mushroom soup
1/2	cup melted butter or margarine
2	cups grated cheddar cheese
1/4	cup grated onion
1/4	cup parmesan cheese

salt and pepper to taste

Thaw potatoes slightly. Mix first 6 ingredients together and place in a 9 X 13 inch baking dish. Sprinkle top with parmesan cheese. Bake at 350 for 1 to 1 1/2 hours.

SLEAZY EASY CHICKEN

4 to 6   medium size chicken breasts
1   can cream of chicken soup
1   cup mushrooms (sliced)
1/2   cup cooking sherry
1/4   cup toasted almond slivers

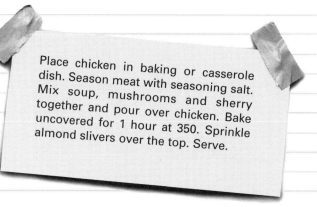

Place chicken in baking or casserole dish. Season meat with seasoning salt. Mix soup, mushrooms and sherry together and pour over chicken. Bake uncovered for 1 hour at 350. Sprinkle almond slivers over the top. Serve.

BACHELOR'S BBQ RIBS

3 pounds baby back ribs
1 cup ketchup
1/2 cup brown sugar
1/4 cup vinegar
1 tsp. seasoning salt
1 tsp. garlic salt
1/2 tsp. hot mustard powder
1 tsp. Worcestershire sauce

Combine all ingredients and brush over ribs while cooking. Also, great on burgers, chicken or steak. Enjoy.

Magic Mushroom Rice Pilaf

1	cup rice
2	cups mushrooms (diced)
2	tbsp. butter
1/4	cup chicken stock
2	stalks green onion chopped
1	small onion finely chopped
1/2	tsp. paprika

salt to taste

Boil rice, drain. Combine mushrooms, onion and green onions. Add stock and combine with rice, paprika and salt to taste. Place in casserole dish and cook for 40 to 50 minutes at 350 degrees. Serve.

LECTURE LASAGNA

1	pound lasagna noodles (cooked)
3/4	pound ground beef
3/4	pound ground pork
3/4	cup onion (chopped)
1	clove garlic (crushed)
1	tsp. parsley
2	cups water
2	small cans tomato paste
1/2	tsp. pepper
1	tsp. salt
1	pound mozzarella cheese
1	pound ricotta cheese
1/2	cup romano cheese

Cook beef and pork together in a large sauce pan until browned. Add onion, garlic, parsley, water, tomato paste, salt and pepper. Simmer for 15 minutes.

To assemble lasagna:
Grease a large baking dish, and spread a thin layer of sauce on the bottom. Then put down a layer of the cooked lasagna noodles-over-lapping them slightly. Add a layer of mozzarella and ricotta cheese and a generous amount of sauce. Top the cheese and sauce layer with another layer of noodles and then repeat this process until all of the layers are completed. Add the grated romano cheese to the top of the final layer. Bake at 350 degrees for 45 minutes. Let cool for 10 minutes before serving.

UPPER CLASS HASH

1	pound ground beef
2	medium onions (chopped)
1	cup celery (chopped)
1	can mushroom soup
1	can cream of chicken soup
1 1/2	cups warm water
1/2	cup rice (uncooked)
1/4	cup soya sauce
1	can crisp chow mein noodles

salt and pepper to taste

Brown hamburger and onions together. Combine with all other ingredients except chow mein noodles in a large casserole dish and bake at 300 degrees for 30 minutes. Remove cover, top with chow mein noodles and bake for another 15 minutes.

DINNER IN A DISH

1	chuck roast (3 1/2 pounds)
1	can cream of celery soup
1/2	pkg. onion soup mix
4	large potatoes (peeled and cut-up)
4	large carrots (peeled and sliced)
8	stalks of celery (chopped)
1/4	pounds fresh mushrooms
1/2	cup red wine

Place roast in a large casserole dish and top with the cream of celery soup. Sprinkle onion soup mix over roast. Place cut-up potatoes and carrots around roast and bake at 350 degrees for 1 hour. Then add celery, mushrooms and wine. Bake for 1 hour more.

HOLY COW CASSEROLE

2	pounds beef steak (cut in 1 1/2 inch cubes)
1	can consomme soup
1	can cream of mushroom soup
1	tsp. Worcestershire sauce
1	pkg. frozen green beans
1	can mushrooms

Mix beef steak, consomme, mushroom soup, and Worcestershire sauce in a large casserole dish. Cover dish and bake at 350 degrees for 2 hours. Add the rest of ingredients and bake for another hour at 300 degrees. Serve on rice or egg noodles.

Sloppy Joe's

1	pound ground beef
1/2	cup sweet relish
1	small onion (diced)
1	can sliced mushrooms
1	can tomato soup

Brown ground beef and onion. Remove excess fat and add all remaining ingredients. Simmer for 30 minutes. Serve on hamburger buns.

CHAMPION CHOPS

6   pork chops
3   eggs (beaten)
1   cup bread crumbs
1   can tomato soup
1/4 cup vinegar
1/2 cup brown sugar
1/2 tsp. allspice
1/2 tsp. cloves
salt and pepper to taste

Dip pork chops in egg and then roll in bread crumbs. Brown chops in frying pan in a little oil. In a sauce pan, bring tomato soup, vinegar, brown sugar, cloves, and spices to a boil. Place chops in a greased baking dish and cover with sauce. Bake uncovered at 350 degrees for 1 hour.

HOT'N HONEY CHICKEN

1   small roasting chicken (or pieces)
1/3   cup butter
1/2   cup honey
1/4   cup dry mustard
4   tsp. curry powder
1   tsp. soya sauce

Melt butter and stir in all other ingredients and heat over medium heat for 3 to 5 minutes. Place chicken in pan and pour sauce over chicken. Cook for approximately 1 hour at 375 degrees. Serve.

MED STUDENT'S
MACARONI

2 1/2 cups macaroni (cooked)
1 pound ground beef
1 large onion (chopped)
1 can tomato soup
1 can tomato paste
1 can sliced mushrooms
1/2 tsp. oregano
salt and pepper to taste

Brown ground beef and onion. Add rest of ingredients and cook on low heat for 30 minutes. Add cooked macaroni and simmer for another 10 minutes before serving.

FABULOUS FRESHMAN FISH FILLETS

1/2 pound fish fillets
3 tbsp. butter
3 tbsp. slivered almonds
1 tbsp. lemon juice
1/4 tsp. parsley flakes
salt and pepper to taste

Melt butter on low heat, add almonds and cook for 3 minutes. Add lemon juice, parsley flakes and salt and pepper. Place fish fillets in lightly greased pan and pour sauce over fillets. Cook at 350 degrees for approximately 10-15 minutes or until fish is firm to touch. Serve.

Totally Fab!!!

PORK "10" DER LOIN

2 pounds of pork loin (cut into 1" cubes)
4 tbsp. flour
4 tbsp. water
1/4 cup vinegar
2 tbsp. brown sugar
1 can pineapple cubes and juice
salt and pepper to taste

Brown pork loin in a little oil and transfer to a casserole dish. Add vinegar, brown sugar, pineapple and juice. Mix flour and water to form a paste and add to casserole to thicken. Bake at 300 degrees for 2 hours. Serve over rice.

She's a real "10" of a dish.

Simon's Salmon a la Super Simple

4	salmon steaks
1/2	small onion (cut into rings)
2	tbsp. white wine
1	tsp. fresh minced garlic
1	tbsp. olive oil
1/4	cup lemon juice
1 1/2	tsp. mustard (dijon is best)
1/8	tsp. dill weed

Sauté garlic in olive oil over low heat for 3 minutes. Take off the heat and stir in lemon juice, mustard, wine and dill. Place salmon in lightly greased pan, spoon sauce over steaks. Cover with white onion rings and cook for approximately 10 minutes per inch of fish at 350 degrees.

PENCIL PUSHER PORK CASSEROLE

3/4 pounds of cubed cooked ham
1 small onion (minced)
4 small potatoes (thinly sliced)
3 tbsp. flour
1/2 tsp. salt
1/4 tsp. pepper
1 cup grated cheddar cheese
1 cup milk
2 tbsp. butter
1/4 cup ketchup

Grease casserole dish. Layer in potato slices, onion, ham and cheese and sprinkle with flour, salt and pepper. Repeat layering until casserole is full. Heat milk and butter in a sauce pan and pour over casserole. Bake covered at 350 degrees for 1 hour. Then uncover and dot with ketchup and continue to bake for another 30 minutes.

SHE'S SWEET AND HE'S SOUR MEATBALLS

1	pound ground beef
1/2	tsp. salt
1/2	tsp. garlic salt
2	green onions (chopped)
1	small can water chestnuts
1	cup water
1/2	cup brown sugar
1/3	cup vinegar
2	tbsp. soya sauce
1	tbsp. corn starch
	(dissolved in 2 tbsp. water)

Mix together ground beef, salt, garlic salt, green onions and water chestnuts and form into small meatballs. Brown meat balls in a little oil and set aside. Heat together water, brown sugar, vinegar, soya sauce, and corn starch to form a sauce. Mix sauce and meatballs together and simmer for 10-15 minutes.

Midterm Meatloaf

2	pounds ground beef
1	can vegetable soup
1/2	cup bread crumbs
1	tbsp. prepared mustard
1	tsp. salt
1/4	tsp. pepper
1	egg (beaten)
1	onion (chopped)
1	tbsp. Worcestershire sauce

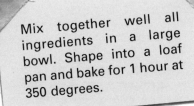

Mix together well all ingredients in a large bowl. Shape into a loaf pan and bake for 1 hour at 350 degrees.

"PANTY RAID" PIZZA

1	large Italian style flat bread
1	small can tomato paste
2	cups mozzarella cheese (grated)
1	can mushrooms (sliced)
1	small green pepper (sliced)
1	small tomato (diced)
1/2	cup pepperoni meat (sliced)
1/4	cup feta cheese
1	tbsp. olive oil
1/2	tsp. oregano

Place flat bread on a cookie sheet. Mix olive oil and tomato paste together and brush over top of bread. Assemble all other ingredients over top of bread. Place under broiler in oven and heat until all cheese is melted. Serve.

GOOD OLD CHAP BATTER

1 cup flour (sifted)
1/2 tsp. salt
1 tbsp. cooking oil
1 tsp. baking powder
1/2 cup milk
1 egg
1 tbsp. vinegar

Sift flour and baking powder together, set aside. In a separate bowl, combine egg, milk, oil and vinegar. Add wet mixture to flour mixture and beat well with wire whisk. Dip fish in batter and deep fry until golden brown.

Great fish and chip batter!!!

DRUNK OLD CHAP BATTER

3/4 cup flour
1/2 tsp. salt
2   eggs (separated)
1/2 cup beer
2   tbsp. melted butter

Sift flour and salt in bowl. Make a well in centre of flour. Beat egg yolks and beer lightly together. Stir in butter and let sit for 30 minutes. Take egg whites and beat until stiff. Fold into batter and mix well. Dip into batter and deep fry until golden brown.

Batter is great on mushrooms, cheese, chicken, onion rings or shrimp or what ever else you find in the refrigerator.

DEADLY BANGIN' BEANS

3	14 ounce cans brown beans
1/2	pound bacon (raw, sliced)
1	medium onion (diced)
1/2	cup ketchup
3	tbsp. brown sugar
1	tsp. hot dry mustard
1	tsp. Worcestershire sauce

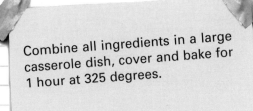

Combine all ingredients in a large casserole dish, cover and bake for 1 hour at 325 degrees.

Great today....
not sure about tomorrow!!

Sophomore Spaghetti

1	pound ground beef
1	large onion (diced)
4	stalks celery (sliced)
1	small green pepper (diced)
1	small can stewing tomatoes
1	can tomato soup
1	small can tomato paste
1	can sliced mushrooms
1/2	tsp. oregano
1/2	tsp. curry powder
1/2	tsp. parsley flakes

parmesan cheese
salt and pepper to taste

In a large frying pan, brown ground beef, onion, celery and green pepper together. Pour off grease. Add mushrooms, stewing tomatoes, soup, tomato paste and dry ingredients. Mix well and simmer over medium heat for 20 to 30 minutes. Cook pasta in lightly oiled water until tender. Mix pasta and sauce together and top with parmesan cheese.

TUTOR TORTELLINI

1	pound fresh tortellini
2	cloves garlic (minced)
2	tbsp. olive oil
1/2	tsp. basil
1	small tomato (diced)
3/4	cup mushrooms (sliced)
3/4	cup heavy cream
1/4	cup parmesan cheese
1/4	tsp. pepper

In a large pan, sauté garlic in olive oil. Add basil, mushrooms and tomato and simmer on medium heat until tomato is soft. Add cream, pepper and cheese and bring to boil until sauce thickens, approximately 4-5 minutes. Cook tortellini in boiling water for 8-10 minutes. Drain. Mix tortellini and sauce together and serve.

HO - LEE - CHOW STIRFRY

1	pound round steak (sliced thinly)
1	crown broccoli
2	cups mushrooms (sliced in quarters)
2	medium tomatoes (sliced in quarters)
1	small onion (sliced in quarters)
2	tbsp. soya sauce
2	tbsp. sherry
1	tbsp. corn starch
1	tsp. sugar

Slice beef into thin pieces and place in bowl. Place soya sauce, sherry, corn starch and sugar on top of meat and mix together. Marinate meat for a minimum 6 to 8 hours. In a large frying pan or wok, place 1 tbsp of oil, add meat while stirring constantly. When meat is cooked, remove from pan. Add onion, broccoli and mushrooms and cook until tender. Add tomatoes. Add back meat to reheat while mixing all ingredients together. Serve immediately over white rice.

MY FAVORITE CUISINE

DESSERTS

PEANUT BUTTER COOKIES

1/2 cup butter
1/2 cup peanut butter
1/2 cup brown sugar
1/2 cup white sugar
1 cup flour
1 egg (beaten)
1 tsp. baking soda
1/8 tsp. salt

Cream together butter, peanut butter, sugar and egg. Sift together flour, salt and baking soda. Mix wet and dry ingredients together. Roll dough into little balls and place onto greased cookie sheet. Press down on each cookie with a fork to flatten. Bake at 350 degrees for 10 to 15 minutes.

BEER BUDDY BREAD

2   cups white all-purpose flour
1   cup whole wheat flour
1   cup grated cheddar cheese
1   bottle beer
1   tbsp. sugar
1   tbsp. baking powder
1   tbsp. dijon mustard
pinch of salt

In a large bowl, combine flour, sugar, salt, baking powder and mix well together. Add in mustard and cheddar cheese. Slowly stir in beer, small amounts at a time, stirring constantly. Place mixture in bread loaf pan and bake for 40-45 minutes at 350 degrees.

Hard to believe....
you can actually do more with beer
than just drink it, go figure!!

FIZZING BISCUITS

2   cups flour
1   tbsp. baking powder
1   tsp. salt
1/3 cup margarine
3/4 cup 7-up soda pop

Mix all dry ingredients together. Mix in margarine until mixture becomes crumbly. Add most of soda pop and continue to mix. Add remaining soda pop to mixture to make dough soft but not too sticky to touch. Knead dough on a flour covered surface for 1 minute. Roll dough out to approximately 1/2 inch of thickness. Cut dough into squares or circles and place on an ungreased cookie sheet. Bake for 12 to 15 minutes at 450 degrees. Should be golden brown prior to taking out of oven. Serve.

"U Go Girl" Squares

1   pkg. butterscotch chips
1   pkg. chocolate chips
1/2 cup butter
3/4 cup peanut butter
3/4 pkg. miniature marshmallows
pinch of salt

In a sauce pan on low heat combine the chips, butter and peanut butter. Melt and stir until smooth. Add a pinch of salt and let mixture cool slightly. Fold in miniature marshmallows and transfer to an 8" square pan. Chill in refrigerator. Cut into squares and serve.

Carrot Muffins

1	cup sugar
1	egg (beaten)
1/2	cup oil
1	tsp. cinnamon
1	tsp. baking soda
1	cup carrots (grated)
1/2	cup shredded coconut
1/2	cup crushed pineapple (drained)
1 1/4	cups all purpose flour
1/2	tsp. salt
1	tsp. vanilla extract

Mix together egg, sugar, baking soda, vanilla, cinnamon and salt. Add oil and mix in flour. Add pineapple, coconut and carrots and mix thoroughly. Place into greased muffin tin and bake at 350 degrees for 20 minutes.

TOMATO BREAD LOAF

1 1/3   cups flour
1   cup sugar
1   cup raisins
1   can tomato soup
1/2   cup margarine
1   tsp. baking soda
1/2   tsp. nutmeg
1/2   tsp. cloves
1/2   tsp. cinnamon

Mix all ingredients together and place mixture in a bread loaf pan. Bake at 325 degrees for 90 minutes.

7 MINUTE QUICKIE COOKIES

1	cup sugar
1/4	cup butter
1/4	cup milk
1/4	tsp. vanilla extract
1 1/2	cup oatmeal
1/2	cup coconut
1/4	cup cocoa

pinch of salt

Combine milk, butter, sugar, cocoa, vanilla, and salt in a saucepan and heat to boiling. Cool mixture and stir in oatmeal and coconut. Drop spoonfuls of the mixture onto waxed paper to cool.

Takes longer to eat them than make them!!

NICE BUNS, BABY

24   frozen dinner rolls
1/2 cup melted butter
1/2 cup brown sugar
1/2 pkg. Instant butterscotch pudding
1   pkg. chopped pecan nuts
1/2 tsp. cinnamon

Place frozen buns in a bundt pan or baking dish. Sprinkle pudding on buns. Melt butter and add sugar. Pour over buns. Sprinkle cinnamon and nuts over top of buns. Place towel over buns and leave out to rise overnight (minimum 8 hours). Bake at 350 degrees for 30 minutes.

You will be told for sure
you got nice buns!!

APPLE & RASPBERRY COBBLER CRISP

5 cups apples (sliced)
1/2 cup raspberries (fresh or frozen)
1 cup brown sugar
1 cup flour
3/4 cup rolled oats
1/2 cup margarine (melted)
1 tsp. cinnamon
1/2 tsp. nutmeg

Place fruit in the bottom of a baking dish. In a separate bowl, mix brown sugar, oats, flour, cinnamon and nutmeg together. Stir in margarine and mix well until mixture becomes crumbly. Pour mixture evenly over the top of fruit. Bake at 350 degrees for 40 to 50 minutes. Serve with ice cream or whipped cream. Yummy.

O Gingersnap Cookies

1 1/2	cups butter
2	cups sugar
2	eggs
1/2	cup molasses
4	cups sifted flour
2	tsp. baking soda
2	tsp. cinnamon
2	tsp. ground cloves
2	tsp. ginger

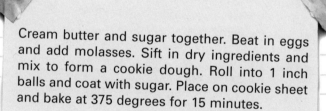

Cream butter and sugar together. Beat in eggs and add molasses. Sift in dry ingredients and mix to form a cookie dough. Roll into 1 inch balls and coat with sugar. Place on cookie sheet and bake at 375 degrees for 15 minutes.

O Ginger, great low fat option...
I'll go tell the Professor!!

SMARTIE PANTS COOKIES

2 1/4 cups all purpose flour
1 1/2 cups Smarties candy
1 cup brown sugar
1/2 cup white sugar
2 eggs
2 tsp. vanilla extract
1 tsp. baking powder
1 tsp. baking soda
1 cup butter

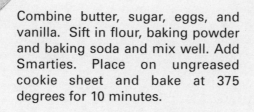

Combine butter, sugar, eggs, and vanilla. Sift in flour, baking powder and baking soda and mix well. Add Smarties. Place on ungreased cookie sheet and bake at 375 degrees for 10 minutes.

Total "Brain Power" food....eat 4 cookies before every exam!!

CHOCOLATE CHIP COOKIES

1/2 cup butter

1/2 cup Crisco shortening

1/2 cup sugar

1/4 cup brown sugar

1 cup flour

1/2 pkg. chocolate chips

1/2 cup chopped walnuts (optional)

1 egg

1 tsp. vanilla extract

1/4 tsp. baking soda

pinch of salt

Cream butter and Crisco with sugar, add egg and mix well. Combine all remaining ingredients to form cookie dough and roll into balls. Bake at 350 degrees for 15 minutes on greased cookie sheet.

CAN'T COOK COOKIES

1 1/4 cups rolled oats
1   egg
1/2   cup butter
1/2   cup brown sugar
1/2   cup sugar
1/2   cup flour
1/2   cup shaved coconut
1/2   tsp. baking soda
1/2   tsp. baking powder
1   tsp. vanilla extract
pinch of salt

Cream butter and sugar together, beat in egg. Combine flour, baking soda, baking powder and salt. Beat dry ingredients into butter mixture. Add vanilla, rolled oats and coconut into mixture. Roll mixture into balls and place on a cookie sheet. Press ball with fork. Bake at 350 degrees for 10 to 15 minutes.

These are sooo easy!!

BANANA MUFFINS

1 1/2 cups flour
3/4 cup sugar
1/2 cup butter (melted)
1 egg
1 tsp baking powder
1 tsp baking soda
3 bananas (mashed)
pinch of salt

Combine all ingredients, mix until smooth. Place mixture in lightly greased muffin tin or paper cups. Bake at 400 degrees for 15 minutes. Makes 12 muffins.

BANANA SPLIT PIE

3	cups Graham wafer crumbs
3	bananas
1	cup strawberries
1	small can crushed pineapple
1	pkg. vanilla pudding
1	container Cool Whip (4 cups)

In a 9 X 12 dish, spread Graham wafer crumbs over bottom and press firm down into a even layer. In an separate bowl, mix vanilla pudding together and then place over Graham wafer layer. Peel and slice bananas length wise. Place each slice width wise in pan over pudding. Spread strawberries and crushed pineapple evenly over bananas. Top with a thick layer of Cool Whip. Cover and place in freezer. 1 hour before serving, remove from freezer to thaw, top with crushed walnuts and cherries. Cut into squares and serve.

MY FAVORITE DESSERTS

BAKED APPLES

3   apples (peeled and cored)
1/2   cup raisins
1/2   cup brown sugar
1/2   cup water
2   tbsp. butter
1/4   tsp. nutmeg
1/4   tsp. cinnamon

Place apples in a deep baking pan. Fill each apple with a handful of raisins. Bring brown sugar, water, butter, nutmeg and cinnamon to a boil. Pour sauce over apples. Bake at 350 degrees for 1 hour. Baste apples every 15 minutes.

PREPPIE POPCORN BALLS

3   quarts sugar
1   cup sugar
1/3   cup corn syrup
1/3   cup water
1/4   cup butter
3/4   tsp. salt
3/4   tsp. vanilla

Make popcorn and keep hot in oven. Combine sugar, corn syrup, water, butter and salt and heat until sugar is dissolved. Continue cooking without stirring (approximately 270 degrees) until syrup begins to bubble. Test syrup by dripping a small amount into cold water. If ready, syrup will form brittle balls. Remove from heat and stir in vanilla. Pour mixture over popcorn. Mix well. To form balls, grease hands with butter, and roll popcorn into medium size balls.

BACHELOR'S BROWNIES

1/2 cup flour
1/2 cup unsweetened cocoa powder
1/4 tsp. salt
2 egg whites
1 egg
3/4 cup sugar
6 tbsp. unsweetened applesauce
2 tbsp. vanilla extract
1 tbsp. chopped walnuts (optional)

In a medium bowl, combine flour, cocoa and salt. Mix well. In another larger bowl, whisk together egg whites, egg, sugar, applesauce, oil and vanilla. Stir in flour mixture. Mix well but do not over mix. Coat an 8 inch baking pan with cooking spray and pour batter into pan. Bake at 350 degrees for approximately 25 minutes. Check with the "toothpick" test to ensure brownies are totally cooked. Let cool for 15 minutes. Cut into 12 squares and enjoy.

CRUNCHY GRANOLA

4	cups rolled oats
1 1/2	cups walnuts (chopped)
1	cup raisins
1	cup almonds (slivered)
1	cup coconut (shaved)
1	cup oil
1/2	cup sunflower seeds
1/2	cup liquid honey
1/2	cup wheat germ
2	tbsp. milk
1	tsp. vanilla extract
1/2	tsp. salt

Mix all dry and wet ingredients together in separate bowls. Mix wet ingredients into dry ingredients and stir well together. Place in a medium size baking dish and bake at 350 degrees for 30 minutes. Stir mixture while cooking. Let cool before serving.

If you like hugging trees...
you'll love eating this!

PUFF N STUFF WHEAT SQUARES

4 cups puffed wheat
1/2 cup brown sugar
1/4 cup corn syrup
2 tbsp cocoa powder
2 tbsp butter or margarine

Bring sugar, corn syrup, cocoa powder and butter to a boil for approximately 3-5 minutes. Remove from heat and stir in puffed wheat. Place mixture in a 9 X 12 pan, pressing mixture into all corners. Let cool and enjoy.

NUTS & JOLTS

1/2 box Cheerios cereal
1/2 box Life cereal
1/2 box Shreddies cereal
1 box salted pretzel sticks
1 can salted peanuts
1 can cashew nuts
1 pkg. ranch salad dressing mix
1/2 cup oil
2 tsp. dill weed
1/2 tsp. garlic powder

In a saucepan, combine oil, dill, garlic powder and salad dressing mix. Stir together over medium heat. In a large separate bowl, combine all cereals, pretzels, and nuts together. Drizzle sauce over mixture, stirring constantly until all sauce is absorbed. Let cool and serve.

Give yourself a handful of Jolts!!

VARSITY VEGGIE DIP

2 1/2   cups mayonnaise
3   tbsp. ketchup
1   tsp. Worcestershire sauce
1   tsp. curry powder

Combine all ingredients, blend well and refrigerate.

SO-SO SOPHISTICATED SALAD DRESSING

1/4   cup sugar
1   cup vegetable oil
2 1/2   tbsp vinegar
1   tsp dry mustard
1   small red onion (minced)

Combine all ingredients and refrigerate. Drizzle dressing over fruit or garden salad prior to serving.

FABULOUS FUDGE

1/2 cup margarine
3   tbsp. boiling water
4   cups icing sugar
3   squares of semi sweet chocolate
1   tsp. vanilla extract
1/2 cup crushed walnuts (optional)

Melt chocolate and margarine together in a double boiler. Add boiling water and stir in icing sugar, vanilla extract and walnuts. Once all mixed together, pour mixture on a 8" X 8" greased pan. Let stand until cool. Cut into squares and serve.

KAPPA KARMEL SAUCE

1 1/2   cups brown sugar
3 1/2   tsp. flour
2   tsp. butter
1-1 1/2 cups water
1   tbsp. vanilla extract

Place brown sugar and flour in a pot. Add butter and heat until sugar melts. Add water and heat til sauce thickens. Remove from heat and add vanilla. Stir well. Serve over cake, ice cream or pudding.

NAUGHTY NACHOS

1   pkg. nacho chips
1   cup cheese (grated)
1   small tomato (diced)
3   green onions (sliced)
12   black olives (sliced)
1/4   cup sliced jalapeno peppers (optional)

Spread nachos out over a cookie sheet. Sprinkle cheese, tomato, green onions and black olives over the nachos. Broil for 4-5 minutes. Serve with sour cream, salsa, and/ or guacamole.

MY FAVORITE MUNCHIES

BAR & BEVERAGES

Isabell's Drink

6	large strawberries
1	tsp strawberry juice
1 1/4	ounces rum
2	scoops vanilla ice cream
2	cups ice cubes
splash	lime juice

Place all ingredients in a blender, blend well, pour in brandy snifter glass. Garnish with strawberry on toothpick.

Margarita

1/2	ounce Tequila
1/2	ounce Triple Sec
6 to 8	ounces lime juice
6	ice cubes

Mix above in blender until smooth. Serve in salt rimmed margarita glass. Garnish with a lime wedge.

ZOMBIE

1 ounce dark rum
1 ounce white rum
1/4 ounce amber rum
1/2 ounce orange juice
1/4 ounce lime juice
1/4 ounce lemon juice
splash of apricot brandy

Beginning with liquor, layer all ingredients in a tall glass over ice. Mix well. Garnish with orange and cherry on toothpick.

DREAMSICLE

1/2 ounce vodka
1/2 ounce Kahlua
1/4 ounce Triple Sec
6 ice cubes

Combine all ingredients in a blender. Serve.

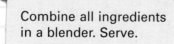

Summer Slush

24	ounces white rum
10	ounces Wink soda pop
2	cans frozen limeade
2	cans frozen lemonade
1	large bottle 7-up

Mix all ingredients well and place in freezer for a minimum of 6 hours. The mixture will not freeze solidly, but will remain "slushy" until ready to serve. Enjoy!

Planter's Punch

1	ounce rum
1	ounce orange juice
1	ounce lime juice
1	ounce lemon juice

top with 7-up

Blend well and pour over crushed ice.

PINK GIN PUNCH

25 ounces gin
4 ounces Cherry brandy
4 ounce pineapple juice
8 ounces orange juice
8 ounces lemon juice
4 ounces berry sugar
2 ounces grenadine
20 ounces ginger ale

Combine all ingredients; pour into punch bowl over ice cubes.

GRASSHOPPER

1/2 ounce Creme de Menthe (green)
1/2 ounce Creme de Cacao (white)
6 ice cubes
splash of milk

Combine all ingredients and blend well in blender.

RUDY ROOTBEER

1   ounce Kahlua
1/4   ounce Galliano
3/4   ounce soda
1/4   ounce coke

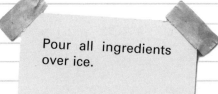

Pour all ingredients over ice.

TEQUILA SUNRISE

1   ounce Tequila
6   ounces orange juice
dash of grenadine

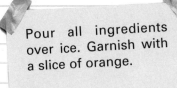

Pour all ingredients over ice. Garnish with a slice of orange.

DAIQUIRI

1	ounce white rum
1/4	ounce Triple Sec
6	ounces lime juice
1	cup fresh fruit
6	ice cubes

Place all ingredients in a blender. Blend well and pour in glass. Garnish with orange slice and cherry on toothpick.

PINA COLADA

1	ounce white rum
6	ounces pineapple juice
1/2	ounce coconut syrup
6	ice cubes
	splash of milk

Place all ingredients in blender. Blend well and pour in glass. Garnish with slice of pineapple.

CHI-CHI

1 ounce vodka
6 ounces pineapple juice
1/2 ounce coconut syrup
6 ice cubes
splash of milk

Place all ingredients in blender. Blend well and pour in glass. Garnish with slice of pineapple.

SPANISH COFFEE

1 ounce Tia Maria
1 ounce brandy
1 cup hot coffee
1 tsp sugar

Dip edge of glass in lemon juice and sugar. Combine all ingredients in brandy snifter glass. Top with whip cream. Garnish with cherry.

HOT RUM FOR THE TUM

1/2 cup melted butter
2 cups brown sugar
1/2 tsp nutmeg
1/2 tsp cloves
1/2 tsp cinnamon

Mix above ingredients into a paste. Add 1 1/2 ounces rum with one heaping tbsp of mixture into a cup. Add boiling water and stir well. Place remaining mixture in the fridge until next time. Garnish with a cinnamon stick.

CAPPUCCINO

3 cups hot coffee (double strength)
3 cups boiling milk
dash of cinnamon sugar
dash of nutmeg

Pour all ingredients in 4 cups, sprinkle with cinnamon sugar and nutmeg. Add sugar to taste.

SPICE BOYS ICED CAFE

2   tbsp. instant coffee

4   cups boiling water

2   slices ginger root (sliced)

1/2 cup coffee creamer

1/4 cup brown sugar

1/4 cup coconut rum

Ice

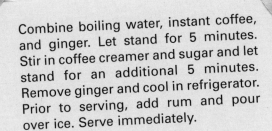

Combine boiling water, instant coffee, and ginger. Let stand for 5 minutes. Stir in coffee creamer and sugar and let stand for an additional 5 minutes. Remove ginger and cool in refrigerator. Prior to serving, add rum and pour over ice. Serve immediately.

Super Sexy Sangria

1/2 cup iced tea mix
3 cups dry red wine
2 cups sparkling mineral water
1 cup orange juice
2 tbsp. orange liqueur
slices of orange, lemon and lime

Place iced tea mix in a large pitcher. Stir in wine, sparkling mineral water, orange juice and orange liqueur. Stir until iced tea mix is dissolved. Add slices of orange, lemon and lime. Fill pitcher with ice. Serve.

SHOOTER LIST

Jelly Bean
1/8 ounce grenadine
1/2 Anisette
1/2 ounce Southern Comfort

B-52
1/4 ounce Kahlua
1/4 ounce Baileys
1/4 ounce Grand Marnier

After Eight
1/3 ounce Kahlua
1/3 ounce Creme de Menthe (green)
1/3 ounce milk

Money's Lunch
1/4 ounce Kahlua
1/4 ounce banana liquor
1/4 ounce Baileys

Coma
1/3 ounce Kahlua
1/3 ounce Anisette
1/3 ounce Grand Marnier

MY FAVORITE DRINK

INDEX

Soups, Salads and Sandwiches

Stuff Your Face Cuisine

Desserts

Munchies

Bar and Beverages

MATH 101 FORMULAS

Volumes	Weight	Oven Temp
1/4 tsp. = 1 ml.	1 oz. = 30 g.	250 F = 120 C
1/2 tsp. = 2 ml.	2 oz. = 55 g.	275 F = 140 C
1 tsp. = 5 ml.	3 oz. = 85 g.	300 F = 150 C
1 tbsp. = 15 ml.	4 oz. = 115 g.	325 F = 160 C
1/4 cup = 60 ml.	5 oz. = 140 g.	350 F = 180 C
1/3 cup = 75 ml.	6 oz. = 170 g.	375 F = 190 C
1/2 cup = 125 ml.	7 oz. = 200 g.	400 F = 200 C
2/3 cup = 150 ml.	8 oz. = 250 g.	425 F = 220 C
3/4 cup = 175 ml.	16 oz. = 500 g.	450 F = 230 C
1 cup = 250 ml.	32 oz. = 1000 g.	475 F = 240 C
		500 F = 260 C

Measurements

3 teaspoons = 1 tablespoon	2 pints = 1 quart
2 tablespoons = 1 fluid ounce	4 quarts = 1 gallon
8 fluid ounces = 1 cup	16 ounces = 1 pound
2 cups = 1 pint	12 inches = 1 foot

To Change

To Change	Into	Multiply by
inches	centimetres	2.5
ounces	grams	28
pounds	kilograms	.45
teaspoons	millilitres	5
tablespoons	millilitres	15
fluid ounces	millilitres	30
cups	litres	.24
pints	litres	.47
quarts	litres	.95
gallons	litres	3.8

ORDER RECIPES "ᐱ" REZ

Order Recipes "ᐱ" Rez Cookbook today

Please send:

_____ Copies of Recipes "ᐱ" Rez ($14.95 US/$19.95 Cdn)
_____ Plus $5.00 (Total Order) for postage and handling
_____ Add 7% GST (Canada only)
$_____ is enclosed

Payment by: CHEQUE _____ M.O. _____
Please make Cheques/Money orders payable to Spruce Street Publishing

NAME: _____
ADDRESS: _____
CITY: _____
PROV/STATE: _____ POSTAL/ZIP CODE:_____
Telephone Number (in case we need to contact regarding this order)
(_____) _____ - _____

Ship to:

NAME: _____
ADDRESS: _____
CITY: _____
PROV/STATE: _____ POSTAL/ZIP CODE:_____

Spruce Street Publishing
35D Spruce Street, Toronto, Ontario, M5A 2H8
Tel: 416-922-6017   Fax: 416-922-9105
E-mail: sprucest@idirect.com

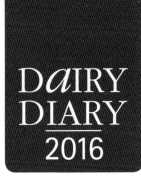

D*a*IRY DIARY
2016

Name	
Address	
Postcode	
📞 Home	
📞 Mobile	
Email	
In case of emergency contact:	
Name	
📞 Tel.	

To contact Eaglemoss, publishers of the Dairy Diary,
ring **01270 270050** or email **enquiries@dairydiary.co.uk**
website: **dairydiary.co.uk**   blog: **dairydiarychat.co.uk**

Year planner 2016

JANUARY	FEBRUARY	MARCH
1 Fri BANK HOLIDAY	**1** Mon	**1** Tue
2 Sat	**2** Tue	**2** Wed
3 Sun	**3** Wed	**3** Thu
4 Mon BANK HOLIDAY SCOTLAND	**4** Thu	**4** Fri
5 Tue	**5** Fri	**5 Sat**
6 Wed	**6 Sat**	**6 Sun**
7 Thu	**7 Sun**	**7** Mon
8 Fri	**8** Mon	**8** Tue
9 Sat	**9** Tue	**9** Wed
10 Sun	**10** Wed	**10** Thu
11 Mon	**11** Thu	**11** Fri
12 Tue	**12** Fri	**12 Sat**
13 Wed	**13 Sat**	**13 Sun**
14 Thu	**14 Sun**	**14** Mon
15 Fri	**15** Mon	**15** Tue
16 Sat	**16** Tue	**16** Wed
17 Sun	**17** Wed	**17** Thu BANK HOLIDAY N IRELAND
18 Mon	**18** Thu	**18** Fri
19 Tue	**19** Fri	**19 Sat**
20 Wed	**20 Sat**	**20 Sun**
21 Thu	**21 Sun**	**21** Mon
22 Fri	**22** Mon	**22** Tue
23 Sat	**23** Tue	**23** Wed
24 Sun	**24** Wed	**24** Thu
25 Mon	**25** Thu	**25** Fri BANK HOLIDAY
26 Tue	**26** Fri	**26 Sat**
27 Wed	**27 Sat**	**27 Sun**
28 Thu	**28 Sun**	**28** Mon BANK HOLIDAY
29 Fri	**29** Mon	**29** Tue
30 Sat		**30** Wed
31 Sun		**31** Thu

2

APRIL	MAY	JUNE
1 Fri	1 Sun	1 Wed
2 Sat	2 Mon BANK HOLIDAY	2 Thu
3 Sun	3 Tue	3 Fri
4 Mon	4 Wed	4 Sat
5 Tue	5 Thu	5 Sun
6 Wed	6 Fri	6 Mon
7 Thu	7 Sat	7 Tue
8 Fri	8 Sun	8 Wed
9 Sat	9 Mon	9 Thu
10 Sun	10 Tue	10 Fri
11 Mon	11 Wed	11 Sat
12 Tue	12 Thu	12 Sun
13 Wed	13 Fri	13 Mon
14 Thu	14 Sat	14 Tue
15 Fri	15 Sun	15 Wed
16 Sat	16 Mon	16 Thu
17 Sun	17 Tue	17 Fri
18 Mon	18 Wed	18 Sat
19 Tue	19 Thu	19 Sun
20 Wed	20 Fri	20 Mon
21 Thu	21 Sat	21 Tue
22 Fri	22 Sun	22 Wed
23 Sat	23 Mon	23 Thu
24 Sun	24 Tue	24 Fri
25 Mon	25 Wed	25 Sat
26 Tue	26 Thu	26 Sun
27 Wed	27 Fri	27 Mon
28 Thu	28 Sat	28 Tue
29 Fri	29 Sun	29 Wed
30 Sat	30 Mon BANK HOLIDAY	30 Thu
	31 Tue	

P.T.O. July-December 2016

Year planner 2016

JULY		AUGUST		SEPTEMBER	
1	Fri	1	Mon — BANK HOLIDAY SCOTLAND	1	Thu
2	Sat	2	Tue	2	Fri
3	Sun	3	Wed	3	Sat
4	Mon	4	Thu	4	Sun
5	Tue	5	Fri	5	Mon
6	Wed	6	Sat	6	Tue
7	Thu	7	Sun	7	Wed
8	Fri	8	Mon	8	Thu
9	Sat	9	Tue	9	Fri
10	Sun	10	Wed	10	Sat
11	Mon	11	Thu	11	Sun
12	Tue — BANK HOLIDAY N IRELAND	12	Fri	12	Mon
13	Wed	13	Sat	13	Tue
14	Thu	14	Sun	14	Wed
15	Fri	15	Mon	15	Thu
16	Sat	16	Tue	16	Fri
17	Sun	17	Wed	17	Sat
18	Mon	18	Thu	18	Sun
19	Tue	19	Fri	19	Mon
20	Wed	20	Sat	20	Tue
21	Thu	21	Sun	21	Wed
22	Fri	22	Mon	22	Thu
23	Sat	23	Tue	23	Fri
24	Sun	24	Wed	24	Sat
25	Mon	25	Thu	25	Sun
26	Tue	26	Fri	26	Mon
27	Wed	27	Sat	27	Tue
28	Thu	28	Sun	28	Wed
29	Fri	29	Mon — BANK HOLIDAY	29	Thu
30	Sat	30	Tue	30	Fri
31	Sun	31	Wed		

OCTOBER	NOVEMBER	DECEMBER
1 Sat	1 Tue	1 Thu
2 Sun	2 Wed	2 Fri
3 Mon	3 Thu	3 Sat
4 Tue	4 Fri	4 Sun
5 Wed	5 Sat	5 Mon
6 Thu	6 Sun	6 Tue
7 Fri	7 Mon	7 Wed
8 Sat	8 Tue	8 Thu
9 Sun	9 Wed	9 Fri
10 Mon	10 Thu	10 Sat
11 Tue	11 Fri	11 Sun
12 Wed	12 Sat	12 Mon
13 Thu	13 Sun	13 Tue
14 Fri	14 Mon	14 Wed
15 Sat	15 Tue	15 Thu
16 Sun	16 Wed	16 Fri
17 Mon	17 Thu	17 Sat
18 Tue	18 Fri	18 Sun
19 Wed	19 Sat	19 Mon
20 Thu	20 Sun	20 Tue
21 Fri	21 Mon	21 Wed
22 Sat	22 Tue	22 Thu
23 Sun	23 Wed	23 Fri
24 Mon	24 Thu	24 Sat
25 Tue	25 Fri	25 Sun
26 Wed	26 Sat	26 Mon BANK HOLIDAY
27 Thu	27 Sun	27 Tue BANK HOLIDAY
28 Fri	28 Mon	28 Wed
29 Sat	29 Tue	29 Thu
30 Sun	30 Wed	30 Fri
31 Mon		31 Sat

Useful NUMBERS

Bank	Hairdresser
Building society	Hospital
Chemist	Milkman
Childminder/nursery/school	National insurance no.
Chiropodist	NHS Direct England 111 Wales 0845 4647 NHS 24 (Scotland) 08454 242424
Council	Optician
Credit card emergency	Pharmacy registration no.
Dentist	Plumber
Doctor	Police station For England and Wales use 101
Electrician	Solicitor
Garage	Taxi
Gas engineer	Veterinary surgery

RENEWAL REMINDERS

	Renewal date	Policy number	Telephone number
Car insurance			
Car tax			
MOT			
Service			
Home insurance			
TV licence			
Other			
Other			

Dairy Diary CONTENTS

40 GROW YOUR OWN TREE

Trees bring a reassuring sense of continuity – plant a tree and in the normal course of events it will be there for generations to come. Growing your own may seem challenging, but choose and position it carefully and your tree will be a glorious reminder of the changing seasons, a haven for wildlife and, generally, a great addition to the garden. Besides this, trees produce oxygen, store carbon dioxide and absorb pollutants, so the more of them the better.

52 QUIRKY PLACES TO STAY

Have you ever considered staying somewhere more unconventional than the usual hotel or B&B – a converted chapel or railway carriage, perhaps? It's not difficult to find a venue offbeat enough to satisfy the wildest craving for the fanciful or eccentric.

Family and FRIENDS

Name

Address

📞 Home

   Work

   Mobile

Email

Name

Address

📞 Home

   Work

   Mobile

Email

Name

Address

📞 Home

   Work

   Mobile

Email

Name

Address

📞 Home

   Work

   Mobile

Email

Name

Address

📞 Home

   Work

   Mobile

Email

Name

Address

📞 Home

   Work

   Mobile

Email

Name

Address

📞 Home

Work

Mobile

Email

Name

Address

📞 Home

Work

Mobile

Email

Name

Address

📞 Home

Work

Mobile

Email

Name

Address

📞 Home

Work

Mobile

Email

Name

Address

📞 Home

Work

Mobile

Email

Name

Address

📞 Home

Work

Mobile

Email

Family and FRIENDS

Name

Address

📞 Home

  Work

  Mobile

Email

Name

Address

📞 Home

  Work

  Mobile

Email

Name

Address

📞 Home

  Work

  Mobile

Email

Name

Address

📞 Home

  Work

  Mobile

Email

Name

Address

📞 Home

  Work

  Mobile

Email

Name

Address

📞 Home

  Work

  Mobile

Email

Name

Address

📞 Home

    Work

    Mobile

Email

Name

Address

📞 Home

    Work

    Mobile

Email

Name

Address

📞 Home

    Work

    Mobile

Email

Name

Address

📞 Home

    Work

    Mobile

Email

Name

Address

📞 Home

    Work

    Mobile

Email

Name

Address

📞 Home

    Work

    Mobile

Email

Home BUDGETING

	JANUARY	FEBRUARY	MARCH
Opening balance			
Income			
New balance			
Birthdays/Christmas			
Car insurance			
Car MOT/service/tax			
Childcare			
Clothing/shoes			
Council tax			
Dentist/optician			
Electricity			
Entertainment			
Gas/oil/solid fuel			
Groceries			
Hairdresser			
Holidays			
Home/pet insurance			
Life/medical insurance			
Mobile/phone/internet			
Mortgage/rent			
Newspapers/magazines			
Petrol/fares			
Pets			
Savings			
TV licence/satellite			
Water rates			
Other			
Other			
Total expenditure			
Closing balance			

	APRIL	MAY	JUNE
Opening balance			
Income			
New balance			
Birthdays/Christmas			
Car insurance			
Car MOT/service/tax			
Childcare			
Clothing/shoes			
Council tax			
Dentist/optician			
Electricity			
Entertainment			
Gas/oil/solid fuel			
Groceries			
Hairdresser			
Holidays			
Home/pet insurance			
Life/medical insurance			
Mobile/phone/internet			
Mortgage/rent			
Newspapers/magazines			
Petrol/fares			
Pets			
Savings			
TV licence/satellite			
Water rates			
Other			
Other			
Total expenditure			
Closing balance			

Home BUDGETING

	JULY	AUGUST	SEPTEMBER
Opening balance			
Income			
New balance			
Birthdays/Christmas			
Car insurance			
Car MOT/service/tax			
Childcare			
Clothing/shoes			
Council tax			
Dentist/optician			
Electricity			
Entertainment			
Gas/oil/solid fuel			
Groceries			
Hairdresser			
Holidays			
Home/pet insurance			
Life/medical insurance			
Mobile/phone/internet			
Mortgage/rent			
Newspapers/magazines			
Petrol/fares			
Pets			
Savings			
TV licence/satellite			
Water rates			
Other			
Other			
Total expenditure			
Closing balance			

	OCTOBER	NOVEMBER	DECEMBER
Opening balance			
Income			
New balance			
Birthdays/Christmas			
Car insurance			
Car MOT/service/tax			
Childcare			
Clothing/shoes			
Council tax			
Dentist/optician			
Electricity			
Entertainment			
Gas/oil/solid fuel			
Groceries			
Hairdresser			
Holidays			
Home/pet insurance			
Life/medical insurance			
Mobile/phone/internet			
Mortgage/rent			
Newspapers/magazines			
Petrol/fares			
Pets			
Savings			
TV licence/satellite			
Water rates			
Other			
Other			
Total expenditure			
Closing balance			

2015

JANUARY
Mon	5	12	19	26
Tue	6	13	20	27
Wed	7	14	21	28
Thu	1	8	15	22	29
Fri	2	9	16	23	30
Sat	3	10	17	24	31
Sun	4	11	18	25

FEBRUARY
Mon	2	9	16	23
Tue	3	10	17	24
Wed	4	11	18	25
Thu	5	12	19	26
Fri	6	13	20	27
Sat	7	14	21	28
Sun	1	8	15	22

MARCH
Mon	2	9	16	23	30
Tue	3	10	17	24	31
Wed	4	11	18	25
Thu	5	12	19	26
Fri	6	13	20	27
Sat	7	14	21	28
Sun	1	8	15	22	29

APRIL
Mon	6	13	20	27
Tue	7	14	21	28
Wed	1	8	15	22	29
Thu	2	9	16	23	30
Fri	3	10	17	24
Sat	4	11	18	25
Sun	5	12	19	26

MAY
Mon	4	11	18	25
Tue	5	12	19	26
Wed	6	13	20	27
Thu	7	14	21	28
Fri	1	8	15	22	29
Sat	2	9	16	23	30
Sun	3	10	17	24	31

JUNE
Mon	1	8	15	22	29
Tue	2	9	16	23	30
Wed	3	10	17	24
Thu	4	11	18	25
Fri	5	12	19	26
Sat	6	13	20	27
Sun	7	14	21	28

JULY
Mon	6	13	20	27
Tue	7	14	21	28
Wed	1	8	15	22	29
Thu	2	9	16	23	30
Fri	3	10	17	24	31
Sat	4	11	18	25
Sun	5	12	19	26

AUGUST
Mon	3	10	17	24	31
Tue	4	11	18	25
Wed	5	12	19	26
Thu	6	13	20	27
Fri	7	14	21	28
Sat	1	8	15	22	29
Sun	2	9	16	23	30

SEPTEMBER
Mon	7	14	21	28
Tue	1	8	15	22	29
Wed	2	9	16	23	30
Thu	3	10	17	24
Fri	4	11	18	25
Sat	5	12	19	26
Sun	6	13	20	27

OCTOBER
Mon	5	12	19	26
Tue	6	13	20	27
Wed	7	14	21	28
Thu	1	8	15	22	29
Fri	2	9	16	23	30
Sat	3	10	17	24	31
Sun	4	11	18	25

NOVEMBER
Mon	2	9	16	23	30
Tue	3	10	17	24
Wed	4	11	18	25
Thu	5	12	19	26
Fri	6	13	20	27
Sat	7	14	21	28
Sun	1	8	15	22	29

DECEMBER
Mon	7	14	21	28
Tue	1	8	15	22	29
Wed	2	9	16	23	30
Thu	3	10	17	24	31
Fri	4	11	18	25
Sat	5	12	19	26
Sun	6	13	20	27

2017

JANUARY
Mon	2	9	16	23	30
Tue	3	10	17	24	31
Wed	4	11	18	25
Thu	5	12	19	26
Fri	6	13	20	27
Sat	7	14	21	28
Sun	1	8	15	22	29

FEBRUARY
Mon	6	13	20	27
Tue	7	14	21	28
Wed	1	8	15	22
Thu	2	9	16	23
Fri	3	10	17	24
Sat	4	11	18	25
Sun	5	12	19	26

MARCH
Mon	6	13	20	27
Tue	7	14	21	28
Wed	1	8	15	22	29
Thu	2	9	16	23	30
Fri	3	10	17	24	31
Sat	4	11	18	25
Sun	5	12	19	26

APRIL
Mon	3	10	17	24
Tue	4	11	18	25
Wed	5	12	19	26
Thu	6	13	20	27
Fri	7	14	21	28
Sat	1	8	15	22	29
Sun	2	9	16	23	30

MAY
Mon	1	8	15	22	29
Tue	2	9	16	23	30
Wed	3	10	17	24	31
Thu	4	11	18	25
Fri	5	12	19	26
Sat	6	13	20	27
Sun	7	14	21	28

JUNE
Mon	5	12	19	26
Tue	6	13	20	27
Wed	7	14	21	28
Thu	1	8	15	22	29
Fri	2	9	16	23	30
Sat	3	10	17	24
Sun	4	11	18	25

JULY
Mon	3	10	17	24	31
Tue	4	11	18	25
Wed	5	12	19	26
Thu	6	13	20	27
Fri	7	14	21	28
Sat	1	8	15	22	29
Sun	2	9	16	23	30

AUGUST
Mon	7	14	21	28
Tue	1	8	15	22	29
Wed	2	9	16	23	30
Thu	3	10	17	24	31
Fri	4	11	18	25
Sat	5	12	19	26
Sun	6	13	20	27

SEPTEMBER
Mon	4	11	18	25
Tue	5	12	19	26
Wed	6	13	20	27
Thu	7	14	21	28
Fri	1	8	15	22	29
Sat	2	9	16	23	30
Sun	3	10	17	24

OCTOBER
Mon	2	9	16	23	30
Tue	3	10	17	24	31
Wed	4	11	18	25
Thu	5	12	19	26
Fri	6	13	20	27
Sat	7	14	21	28
Sun	1	8	15	22	29

NOVEMBER
Mon	6	13	20	27
Tue	7	14	21	28
Wed	1	8	15	22	29
Thu	2	9	16	23	30
Fri	3	10	17	24
Sat	4	11	18	25
Sun	5	12	19	26

DECEMBER
Mon	4	11	18	25
Tue	5	12	19	26
Wed	6	13	20	27
Thu	7	14	21	28
Fri	1	8	15	22	29
Sat	2	9	16	23	30
Sun	3	10	17	24	31

2016

JANUARY

Mon		4	11	18	25
Tue		5	12	19	26
Wed		6	13	20	27
Thu		7	14	21	28
Fri	1	8	15	22	29
Sat	2	9	16	23	30
Sun	3	10	17	24	31

FEBRUARY

Mon	1	8	15	22	29
Tue	2	9	16	23	
Wed	3	10	17	24	
Thu	4	11	18	25	
Fri	5	12	19	26	
Sat	6	13	20	27	
Sun	7	14	21	28	

MARCH

Mon		7	14	21	28
Tue	1	8	15	22	29
Wed	2	9	16	23	30
Thu	3	10	17	24	31
Fri	4	11	18	25	
Sat	5	12	19	26	
Sun	6	13	20	27	

APRIL

Mon		4	11	18	25
Tue		5	12	19	26
Wed		6	13	20	27
Thu		7	14	21	28
Fri	1	8	15	22	29
Sat	2	9	16	23	30
Sun	3	10	17	24	

MAY

Mon		2	9	16	23	30
Tue		3	10	17	24	31
Wed		4	11	18	25	
Thu		5	12	19	26	
Fri		6	13	20	27	
Sat		7	14	21	28	
Sun	1	8	15	22	29	

JUNE

Mon		6	13	20	27
Tue		7	14	21	28
Wed	1	8	15	22	29
Thu	2	9	16	23	30
Fri	3	10	17	24	
Sat	4	11	18	25	
Sun	5	12	19	26	

JULY

Mon		4	11	18	25
Tue		5	12	19	26
Wed		6	13	20	27
Thu		7	14	21	28
Fri	1	8	15	22	29
Sat	2	9	16	23	30
Sun	3	10	17	24	31

AUGUST

Mon	1	8	15	22	29
Tue	2	9	16	23	30
Wed	3	10	17	24	31
Thu	4	11	18	25	
Fri	5	12	19	26	
Sat	6	13	20	27	
Sun	7	14	21	28	

SEPTEMBER

Mon		5	12	19	26
Tue		6	13	20	27
Wed		7	14	21	28
Thu	1	8	15	22	29
Fri	2	9	16	23	30
Sat	3	10	17	24	
Sun	4	11	18	25	

OCTOBER

Mon		3	10	17	24	31
Tue		4	11	18	25	
Wed		5	12	19	26	
Thu		6	13	20	27	
Fri		7	14	21	28	
Sat	1	8	15	22	29	
Sun	2	9	16	23	30	

NOVEMBER

Mon		7	14	21	28
Tue	1	8	15	22	29
Wed	2	9	16	23	30
Thu	3	10	17	24	
Fri	4	11	18	25	
Sat	5	12	19	26	
Sun	6	13	20	27	

DECEMBER

Mon		5	12	19	26
Tue		6	13	20	27
Wed		7	14	21	28
Thu	1	8	15	22	29
Fri	2	9	16	23	30
Sat	3	10	17	24	31
Sun	4	11	18	25	

Calendar DATES

UK HOLIDAYS†

	2016	2017
New Year	Jan 1	Jan 2*
New Year (Scotland)	Jan 1/4*	Jan 2/3*
St Patrick's Day (Northern Ireland)	Mar 17	Mar 17
Good Friday	Mar 25	Apr 14
Easter Monday (except Scotland)	Mar 28	Apr 17
Early Spring	May 2	May 1
Spring	May 30	May 29
Battle of the Boyne (Northern Ireland)	Jul 12	Jul 12
Summer (Scotland)	Aug 1	Aug 7
Summer (except Scotland)	Aug 29	Aug 28
Christmas Day	Dec 27*	Dec 25
Boxing Day	Dec 26	Dec 26

NOTABLE DATES

Burns' Night	Jan 25
Holocaust Memorial Day	Jan 27
Accession of Queen Elizabeth II	Feb 6
Chinese New Year/Year of the Monkey	Feb 8
Shrove Tuesday (Pancake Day)	Feb 9
St Valentine's Day	Feb 14
St David's Day (Wales)	Mar 1
Mothering Sunday	Mar 6
Commonwealth Day	Mar 14
St Patrick's Day (Ireland)	Mar 17
Birthday of Queen Elizabeth II	Apr 21
St George's Day (England)	Apr 23
World Red Cross/Red Crescent Day	May 8
Coronation Day	Jun 2
Queen's Official Birthday (tbc)	Jun 11
Father's Day	Jun 19
Armed Forces' Day	Jun 25
St Swithin's Day	Jul 15
International Day of Peace	Sep 21
United Nations Day	Oct 24
Halloween	Oct 31
Armistice Day	Nov 11
Remembrance Sunday	Nov 13
Birthday of the Prince of Wales	Nov 14
St Andrew's Day (Scotland)	Nov 30

RELIGIOUS DATES

Christian

Epiphany	Jan 6
Ash Wednesday	Feb 10
Palm Sunday	Mar 20
Good Friday	Mar 25
Easter Day	Mar 27
Ascension Day	May 5
Whit Sunday, Pentecost	May 15
Trinity Sunday	May 22
Corpus Christi	May 26
Advent Sunday	Nov 27
Christmas Day	Dec 25

Buddhist

Parinirvana Day	Feb 8
Wesak (Buddha Day)	May 20
Bodhi Day (Buddha's enlightenment)	Dec 8

Hindu

Maha Shivaratri	Mar 8
Holi	Mar 23
Navaratri begins	Oct 1
Diwali begins (also celebrated by Sikhs)	Oct 30

Islamic

Ramadan begins	Jun 7
Eid Ul-Fitr	Jul 5
Eid Ul-Adha	Sep 11
Al-Hijra (New Year)	Oct 2
Milad un Nabi (Prophet's birthday)	Dec 12

Jewish

Purim begins	Mar 24
Pesach (Passover) begins	Apr 23
Shavuot (Pentecost) begins	Jun 12
Rosh Hashanah (Jewish New Year)	Oct 3
Yom Kippur (Day of Atonement)	Oct 12
Succoth (Tabernacles) begins	Oct 17
Chanukah begins	Dec 25

Sikh

These dates follow the Nanakshahi calendar

Birthday of Guru Gobind Singh	Jan 5
Vaisakhi	Apr 13
Birthday of Guru Nanak	Apr 14
Martyrdom of Guru Arjan Dev	Jun 16
Martyrdom of Guru Tegh Bahadur	Nov 24

Note: Many religious dates are based on the lunar calendar and, therefore, we cannot guarantee their accuracy.

†Bank Holiday dates can change *Substitute Bank Holidays – Scotland's New Year holiday falls on a Friday and Saturday in 2016; Christmas Day falls on a Sunday in 2016; New Year's Day falls on a Sunday in 2017

SUNRISE AND SUNSET TIMES Note: times vary – these are for London

Day	Rise H:M	Set H:M	Day	Rise H:M	Set H:M	Day	Rise H:M	Set H:M	Day	Rise H:M	Set H:M
January			**February**			**March**			**April**		
07	**08:05**	16:09	07	**07:30**	17:00	07	**06:32**	17:52	07	**06:22**	19:45
14	**08:01**	16:19	14	**07:17**	17:13	14	**06:16**	18:04	14	**06:06**	19:56
21	**07:54**	16:30	21	**07:04**	17:25	21	**06:00**	18:16	21	**05:52**	20:08
28	**07:46**	16:42	28	**06:49**	17:38	28	**06:44**	19:28	28	**05:37**	20:19
May			**June**			**July**			**August**		
07	**05:21**	20:34	07	**04:45**	21:14	07	**04:53**	21:18	07	**05:34**	20:37
14	**05:10**	20:45	14	**04:43**	21:19	14	**05:00**	21:12	14	**05:45**	20:24
21	**05:00**	20:55	21	**04:43**	21:22	21	**05:09**	21:04	21	**05:56**	20:10
28	**04:52**	21:04	28	**04:46**	21:21	28	**05:19**	20:54	28	**06:07**	19:55
September			**October**			**November**			**December**		
07	**06:23**	19:33	07	**07:12**	18:24	07	**07:05**	16:23	07	**07:52**	15:52
14	**06:34**	19:16	14	**07:23**	18:09	14	**07:17**	16:12	14	**07:59**	15:52
21	**06:45**	19:00	21	**07:35**	17:54	21	**07:29**	16:03	21	**08:04**	15:54
28	**06:57**	18:44	28	**07:48**	17:40	28	**07:40**	15:57	28	**08:06**	15:59

PHASES OF THE MOON

● New moon		) First quarter	
Day	H:M	Day	H:M
Jan 10	01:31	Jan 16	23:26
Feb 8	14:39	Feb 15	07:46
Mar 9	01:54	Mar 15	17:03
Apr 7	11:24	Apr 14	03:59
May 6	19:30	May 13	17:02
Jun 5	03:00	Jun 12	08:10
Jul 4	11:01	Jul 12	00:52
Aug 2	20:45	Aug 10	18:21
Sep 1	09:03	Sep 9	11:49
Oct 1	00:11	Oct 9	04:33
Oct 30	17:38	Nov 7	19:51
Nov 29	12:18	Dec 7	09:03
Dec 29	06:53		

○ Full moon		(Last quarter	
Day	H:M	Day	H:M
		Jan 2	05:30
Jan 24	01:46	Feb 1	03:28
Feb 22	18:20	Mar 1	23:11
Mar 23	12:01	Mar 31	15:17
Apr 22	05:24	Apr 30	03:29
May 21	21:14	May 29	12:12
Jun 20	11:02	Jun 27	18:19
Jul 19	22:57	Jul 26	23:00
Aug 18	09:27	Aug 25	03:41
Sep 16	19:05	Sep 23	09:56
Oct 16	04:23	Oct 22	19:14
Nov 14	13:52	Nov 21	08:33
Dec 14	00:06	Dec 21	01:56

SEASONS

	Month	Day	H:M
Vernal equinox			
Spring begins	**Mar**	20	**04:30**
Summer solstice			
Summer begins	**June**	20	**22:34**
Autumnal equinox			
Autumn begins	**Sep**	22	**14:21**
Winter solstice			
Winter begins	**Dec**	21	**10:44**

BRITISH SUMMERTIME

▶ Clocks go forward
1 hour at 1am on
27 March

◀ Clocks go back
1 hour at 2am on
30 October

Websites

bankholidaydates.co.uk
when–is.com
© Crown copyright and/or database rights.
Reproduced by permission of the Controller of
Her Majesty's Stationery Office and the UK
Hydrographic Office

Anniversaries

WEDDINGS

1 Paper	14 Ivory
2 Cotton	15 Crystal
3 Leather	20 China
4 Books	25 Silver
5 Wood	30 Pearl
6 Iron	35 Coral
7 Wool	40 Ruby
8 Bronze	45 Sapphire
9 Copper	50 Gold
10 Tin	55 Emerald
11 Steel	60 Diamond
12 Silk or linen	65 Blue
13 Lace	Sapphire

BIRTHSTONES AND FLOWERS

Month	Birthstone	Flower
January	Garnet	Carnation
February	Amethyst	Violet
March	Aquamarine	Jonquil
April	Diamond	Sweet Pea
May	Emerald	Lily of the Valley
June	Pearl	Rose
July	Ruby	Larkspur
August	Peridot	Gladiolus
September	Sapphire	Aster
October	Opal	Calendula
November	Topaz	Chrysanthemum
December	Turquoise	Narcissus

2016 MILESTONES

950: Battle of Hastings (1066)
800: King John lost crown jewels in the Wash (12 October 1216) and died a week later
500: Birth of Mary I, Bloody Mary (18 February 1516)
400: Death of William Shakespeare in Stratford upon Avon, aged 52, cause unknown (23 April 1616)
350: Great Fire of London (September 1666)
350: Isaac Newton discovered gravity (1666)
300: Birth of Lancelot 'Capability' Brown, landscape gardener and architect (30 August 1716)
300: Royal Artillery (RA), regiment of the British Army, founded (26 May 1716; name first used in 1720)
200: Birth of Charlotte Brontë (21 April 1816)
175: Thomas Cook opened his first travel agency (5 July 1841)
175: China ceded Hong Kong to Britain (20 January 1841)
175: Royal Botanic Gardens,

Kew, opened to the public
100: Cub scouts founded by Lord Baden-Powell (he founded the boy scouts in 1907)
100: Einstein published theory of general relativity (March 1916). His theory of special relativity ($E=mc^2$) published in 1905
100: Birth of Yehudi Menuhin, violinist and conductor, in New York City (22 April 1916). He spent most of his life in England
75: National Service Act (No 2) extended conscription to 'unmarried women and childless widows' between the ages of 20 and 30 (18 December 1941)
50: Football World Cup won by England (July 1966)
50: Severn Bridge opened by the Queen (8 September 1966)
50: North Sea Gas first pumped ashore by BP (4 March 1966)
25: World Wide Web launched as a publicly available service via the Internet (6 August 1991)

BIRTH OF BEATRIX POTTER 150 YEARS

Helen Beatrix Potter, who gave the world Peter Rabbit, Squirrel Nutkin and Jemima Puddle-Duck, was much more than the writer and illustrator of one of the most successful series of children's books of all time (23 in all). She was also an acclaimed naturalist, scientific illustrator, farmer and breeder of Herdwick sheep. Born in London on 28 July 1866, she went to live in the Lake District after her publisher and fiancé, Norman Warne, died suddenly in 1905. Beatrix took to rural life, buying several farms and working to improve local conditions, including founding a nursing trust. In solicitor William Heelis she found a kindred spirit and, in 1913, they were married. Passionate about preserving the Lake District from developers, she managed land for the National Trust, and left them 15 farms and over 4,000 acres when she died in 1943.

BATTLE OF THE SOMME 100 YEARS

The allied plan was for heavy artillery to pound German positions for a week and then for the infantry to cross the intervening ground to take the vacated trenches. They would continue to advance while the artillery fired over their heads to chase the enemy from the land ahead. But the initial pounding failed to clear the trenches – the soldiers dug in and waited for the barrage to stop – and, on 1 July 1916, the advancing infantry were mown down in no-man's-land. The battle descended into stalemate and in October heavy rain turned the whole region into a muddy nightmare. By the time a halt was called on 18 November, the allies had gained an area roughly 25 miles (40 km) long by 6 miles (9.6 km) wide at the cost of a million casualties, half of them German. The battle had a profound impact on British society. Many of the troops were volunteers. Young men had signed up together and these 'Pals' battalions suffered enormous losses. Now whole communities were left to cope without their 'lost generation'.

SIR FRANCIS CHICHESTER'S VOYAGE AROUND THE WORLD 50 YEARS

On 27 August 1966, at the age of 65, Francis Chichester, navigator, aviator and sailor, set off from Plymouth in his specially built yacht, *Gypsy Moth IV*. His aim was to become the first person to circumnavigate the world solo west to east via the Great Capes (Good Hope, Leeuwin and Horn). When he made it back to Plymouth on 28 May 1967, it was to the acclaim of 250,000 waiting well-wishers. His voyage had taken 226 sailing days, which was faster than the old clipper ships. He was knighted in July 1967.

Websites

beatrixpottersociety.org.uk
britishpathe.com
firstworldwar.com
itnsource.com

Height & weight CHART

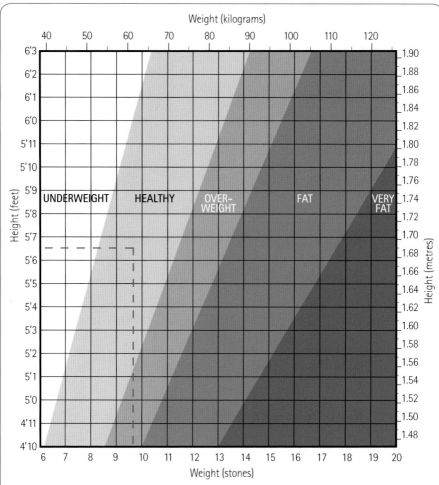

Weight (kilograms)

Height (feet) / Height (metres)

UNDERWEIGHT HEALTHY OVER-WEIGHT FAT VERY FAT

Weight (stones)

Guide for adult men and women

You may need to see your doctor if you are very underweight.	Desirable range for health.	Try to lose weight until you are in the desirable range.	To avoid potential health problems, it is important to lose weight.	Talk to your doctor or practice nurse. You can be referred to a dietitian.

Follow the lines from your weight and height (see example in dotted lines). Where the two figures meet you'll find your weight level.

Metric CONVERSIONS

Length

			To convert	multiply by
1 millimetre (mm)		= 0.0394in	mm to in	0.0394
1 centimetre (cm)	= 10mm	= 0.394in	cm to in	0.394
1 metre (m)	= 100cm	= 1.09yd	m to yd	1.09
1 kilometre (km)	= 1000m	= 0.621 mile	km to mi	0.621
1 inch (in)		= 2.54cm	in to cm	2.54
1 foot (ft)	= 12in	= 30.5cm	ft to cm	30.5
1 yard (yd)	= 3ft	= 0.914m	yd to m	0.914
1 mile (mi)	= 1760yd	= 1.61km	mi to km	1.61

Area

			To convert	multiply by
1 sq millimetre (mm)		= 0.00155sq in	mm^2 to in^2	0.00155
1 sq centimetre (cm)	= 100sq mm	= 0.155sq in	cm^2 to in^2	0.155
1 sq metre (m)	= 10,000sq cm	= 1.20sq yd	m^2 to yd^2	1.20
1 hectare (ha)	= 10,000sq m	= 2.47a	ha to a	2.47
1 sq kilometre (km)	= 100ha	= 0.386sq mile	km^2 to mi^2	0.386
1 sq inch (in)		= 6.45sq cm	in^2 to cm^2	6.45
1 sq foot (ft)	= 144sq in	= 0.0929sq m	ft^2 to m^2	0.0929
1 sq yard (yd)	= 9sq ft	= 0.836sq m	yd^2 to m^2	0.836
1 acre (a)	= 4840sq yd	= 4047sq m	a to m^2	4047
1 sq mile (mi)	= 640a	= 2.59sq km	mi^2 to km^2	2.59

Volume

			To convert	multiply by
1 cu centimetre (cm)	= 1000cu mm	= 0.0611cu in	cm^3 to in^3	0.0611
1 cu decimetre (dm)	= 1000cu cm	= 0.0353cu ft	dm^3 to ft^3	0.0353
1 cu metre (m)	= 1000cu dm	= 1.31cu yd	m^3 to yd^3	1.31
1 cu inch (in)		= 16.4cu cm	in^3 to cm^3	16.4
1 cu foot (ft)	= 1730cu in	= 28.4cu dm	ft^3 to dm^3	28.4
1 cu yard (yd)	= 27cu ft	= 0.765cu m	yd^3 to m^3	0.765

Capacity

			To convert	multiply by
1 millilitre (ml)		= 0.0352fl oz	ml to fl oz	0.0352
1 centilitre (cl)	= 10ml	= 0.352fl oz	cl to fl oz	0.352
1 litre (l)	= 100cl	= 1.76pt	l to pt	1.76
1 fluid ounce (fl oz)		= 28.4ml	fl oz to ml	28.4
1 gill (gi)	= 5fl oz	= 14.2cl	gi to cl	14.2
1 pint (pt)	= 20fl oz	= 0.568l	pt to l	0.568
1 quart (qt)	= 2pt	= 1.14l	qt to l	1.14
1 gallon (gal)	= 4qt	= 4.55l	gal to l	4.55

Weight

			To convert	multiply by
1 gram (g)	= 1000mg	= 0.0353oz	g to oz	0.0353
1 kilogram (kg)	= 1000g	= 2.20lb	kg to lb	2.20
1 tonne (t)	= 1000kg	= 0.984 ton	tonne to ton	0.984
1 ounce (oz)	= 438 grains	= 28.3g	oz to g	28.3
1 pound (lb)	= 16oz	= 0.454kg	lb to kg	0.454
1 stone (st)	= 14lb	= 6.35kg	st to kg	6.35
1 ton (t)	= 160st	= 1.02 tonne	ton to tonne	1.02

Information for COOKS

GRILLING TIMES: FISH

	Minutes each side
Cod (steak)	5–6
Dover sole (fillet)	2–3
Halibut (steak)	5–6
Herring (whole)	4–5
Mackerel (whole)	6–7
Monkfish (steak)	5–6
Plaice (fillet)	2–3
Plaice (whole)	4–6
Salmon (steak)	5–6
Skate	5–6
Tuna (steak)	1–2

Times given for fish weighing approximately 175–225g (6–8oz).

OVEN TEMPERATURES

°C (fan)	°F	Gas	Description
110 (90)	225	¼	cool
120/130 (100/110)	250	½	cool
140 (120)	275	1	very low
150 (130)	300	2	very low
160/170 (140/150)	325	3	low to moderate
180 (160)	350	4	moderate
190 (170)	375	5	moderately hot
200 (180)	400	6	hot
220 (200)	425	7	hot
230 (210)	450	8	hot
240 (220)	475	9	very hot

Guide to recommended equivalent settings, not exact conversions. Always refer to your cooker instruction book.

ROASTING TIMES: MEAT*

Set oven temperature to 180°C/350°F/Gas 4.

	Cooking time per 450g/1lb	Extra cooking time
Beef		
rare	20 min	20 min
medium	25 min	25 min
well done	30 min	30 min
Lamb		
medium	25 min	25 min
well done	30 min	30 min
Pork		
medium	30 min	30 min
well done	35 min	35 min

Let the cooked meat rest for 5–15 minutes before carving to allow the juices to be reabsorbed and to make carving easier.

STEAMING TIMES: VEG

	Minutes
Asparagus	5–7
Beansprouts	3–4
Beetroot (sliced)	5–7
Broccoli (florets)	5–7
Brussels sprouts	5–7
Cabbage (chopped)	4–6
Carrots (thickly sliced)	5–7
Cauliflower (florets)	5–7
Courgettes (sliced)	3–5
Green beans	5–7
Leeks	5–8
Mangetout peas	3–5
Peas	3–5
Potatoes (cubed)	5–7

Times given are for steaming from when water has started to boil.

ROASTING TIMES: POULTRY*

	Oven temperature per 450g/1lb	Cooking time	Extra cooking time	Resting time
Chicken	200°C/400°F/Gas 6	20 min	30 min	15 min
Turkey (stuffed weight)				
small (under 6kg/13lb)	200°C/400°F/Gas 6	12 min	20 min	30 min
large	180°C/350°F/Gas 4	16 min	—	30 min
Duck	200°C/400°F/Gas 6 for 45 min then 180°C/350°F/Gas 4	35 min	—	15 min

* Note that for fan ovens, cooking times are generally reduced by 10 minutes for every hour.

Feel good with DAIRY

A vital aspect of living a healthy life is to consume a balanced diet and within that to include dairy foods. Milk, cheese and yogurt, along with eggs, are among the best sources of protein and calcium – essential nutrients through all stages of life.

As we all know, to keep your body fit and functioning well, there's no getting away from eating healthily and taking plenty of exercise. Of course, knowing what you should do and actually doing it are often two different things but when it comes to the question of diet, dairy foods are a heaven-sent part of the answer. Delicious and versatile, dairy foods can be incorporated into your diet in cooking, snacking and in drinks. They contain vital energy providers – protein, carbohydrates and fats – and also a good slug of essential vitamins and minerals, so you're getting a whole load of nutrients in one hit!

" *Your body contains more calcium than any other mineral* "

CALCIUM

Your body contains more calcium than any other mineral, and most of it is stored in your bones and teeth. Calcium is needed to ensure muscles and nerves work properly, and to aid digestion and blood clotting. Any time levels run a bit low, your body takes what it needs from your bones, so it's important to keep your calcium topped up, or your bone health could be affected.

One of the best ways to do this is to include a good amount of milk, hard cheese and yogurt in your diet because the calcium you get from them is more easily absorbed than from any other source – and they contain protein and phosphorus, which are also good for your bones. Other sources of calcium include oily fish with edible small bones, such

SAMPLE PORTIONS

	calcium content (mg)
Milk (semi-skimmed):	
100ml (half a glass)	124
189ml (third of a pint)	234
284ml (half a pint)	351
200ml (glass)	247
250ml (large glass)	309
Yogurt:	
80g (2 tbsp, whole, plain)	160
125g pot (low-fat, plain)	203
150g pot (low-fat, plain)	243
200g (5 tbsp, low-fat, plain)	324
Hard cheese:	
15g (small cube)	111
20g (2 tbsp, grated)	148
30g (matchbox size, reduced fat)	252
45g (sandwich portion, reduced fat)	378

CALCIUM REQUIREMENTS*

Age	RI** mg/day
1–3	350
4–6	450
7–10	550
11–18 (male)	1000
11–18 (female)	800
19 and over	700

Breastfeeding women should have an extra 550mg/day

*Recommended by the Dairy Council/Department of Health
**Reference Intake. Amounts set by the Department of Health to cover the needs of most people.

as sardines or canned salmon, as well as broccoli, okra and kale, almonds, brazil nuts, hazelnuts, sesame seeds, dried figs and fortified soya.

In order to reap the benefit of all this calcium, though, you must also be getting enough Vitamin D, because this is essential for calcium, as well as several other important minerals, to be absorbed into your system. Vitamin D comes mostly from the action of sunlight on the skin and can be stored in the body, so it's very important for everyone, and particularly children, to spend plenty of time outdoors. Food sources of Vitamin D include oily fish and fortified soya products. The Department of Health recommends that over 65s take a supplement of 10 micrograms of Vitamin D per day.

Too much salt could be a problem since calcium attaches itself to any excess sodium in the body and the two are excreted together. So if you're a salt addict, it could mean that you're unintentionally losing calcium. Adults are recommended to have no more than 6g of salt per day.

FAT

Not all fat is bad! In fact, it's necessary as an energy booster and for the fat-soluble vitamins (A, D, E, K) to function. The harmful effects of too much saturated fat are well known, but one naturally occurring fat found in milk, cheese and yogurt – Conjugated Linoleic Acid (CLA) – is positively beneficial, boosting the immune system and protecting against heart disease and some cancers. And, according to a study conducted by Cambridge University and the Medical Research Council, there is evidence that the saturated fats in dairy foods may protect against type 2 diabetes.

The fat content of cheese varies but the nutritional benefits are beyond doubt, and you can, if you wish, buy reduced-fat versions, so don't deny yourself. A small amount of cheese will only enhance your diet.

Websites

findmeamilkman.net
milk.co.uk

Perfect your technique

PIZZA

A pizza base is primarily a platform for savoury ingredients. If you bake your own, you can make your bases as thick or thin, large or small as you like, and choose your favourite toppings.

"The more vigorous you are the better the dough will be "

P izza has become a perennial favourite of children and adults alike – a meal the whole family can share and enjoy. The first pizzas as we know them probably came from Naples, where they were the staple food of the poor folk who lived and worked around the waterfront, and when migrants from there headed to New York in the 19th century, naturally enough, they took their favourite food with them. Pizzas were a big hit in America and pretty soon pizza parlours were everywhere. The first was Lombardi's in Manhattan, which has been licensed to sell pizza since 1905.

Once the Americans had cottoned on to this easy-eating food, they let their imaginations run wild with the toppings and these days anything goes. Traditional Neapolitan pizzas are much simpler – fresh tomatoes made into a sauce, sliced mozzarella, fresh basil and extra virgin olive oil. The story goes that when Queen Margherita visited Naples in 1889 she loved the local speciality and ever since then, pizza with this topping has been called a Margherita.

Instead of calling for a take-away, why not make your own pizza? It can be great fun for all the family and you get to make it the way you like it.

INGREDIENTS
....
Plain white flour 175g (6oz)
Salt 1/4 tsp
Fast-action dried yeast 1 tsp
Hand-hot water 150ml (1/4 pint)
Olive oil 1 tbsp

EQUIPMENT
....
Oiled baking sheets or pizza stones

MAKING PIZZA DOUGH

1 Mix flour, salt and yeast together in a warm bowl. Make a well in the centre and add warm water and olive oil. Using your hands or a wooden spoon, mix to a soft dough.
2 Turn dough out onto a lightly floured surface and knead for 5 minutes until it is smooth and elastic. The more vigorous you are the better the dough will be.
3 Return ball of dough to the bowl, cover with clingfilm or a damp tea-towel and leave in a warm place until it has doubled in size – about an hour.
4 Preheat oven to 220°C(200°fan)/425°F/Gas 7 and put lightly oiled baking

sheets or pizza stones into oven. Turn dough onto a floured surface and knead for 2–3 minutes. Divide dough in two and roll out to make two 20.5cm (8in) diameter circles and place on heated baking sheets or pizza stones.
5 Carefully crimp up edges of the pizza bases to stop the toppings falling off. Brush tops of the pizzas with oil, cover and leave to stand in a warm place for 10 minutes before covering with tomato sauce and toppings of your choice and baking for 20–25 minutes until they are cooked through and bubbling.

COOK'S TIPS

■ If you are in a hurry, use a packet of pizza-base mix but substitute 1 tbsp of olive oil for some of the warm water to improve the flavour. Knead for 5 minutes, then let the dough sit for just 10 minutes before baking.
■ Don't use water that is more than hand-hot, or you may kill the yeast.
■ Preheating the baking tray or pizza stone results in a good, crispy base.

Time 40 mins plus proving	Makes 2 pizzas Calories 372	Fat 1.7g of which 0.2g is saturated	V

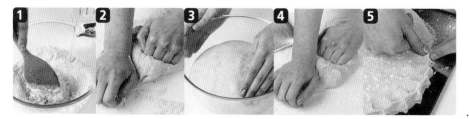

Perfect your technique

ROULADE

A light meringue rolled around a filling of flavoured whipped cream and fresh raspberries makes an attractive and delicious dessert.

A meringue roulade is very similar to a Pavlova except that it's baked in a thin sheet and then filled and rolled up. When you take the cooked rectangle of meringue from the oven, it is hard to believe that it will ever roll up, but with canny use of baking parchment it's not difficult. Just don't overcook the meringue or the crust will become too hard to roll and will taste chewy – and remember that a few cracks will prove the roulade is home-made!

You can make the meringue up to 24 hours in advance, but for the nicest texture, don't fill it until shortly before your guests arrive. Trim off both ends before serving – one of the cook's perks is tasting those trimmings in the kitchen beforehand!

MAKING THE MERINGUE

1 Preheat oven to 150°C(130°fan)/300°F/Gas 2. Line a non-stick Swiss roll tin with lightly oiled baking paper or kitchen foil, leaving a 5cm (2in) overhang all round.
2 Whisk egg whites in a large clean bowl until they are stiff. Gradually whisk in sugar, a little at a time, until mixture is stiff and glossy.

INGREDIENTS

For the meringue
Egg whites 5
Caster sugar 150g (5oz)
Cornflour 2 tsp
Vanilla extract 1 tsp
White wine vinegar 1 tsp
Icing sugar or caster sugar for dusting

Mint sprigs, optional

For the filling
Double cream 284ml carton
Vanilla extract 1 tsp
Icing sugar 50g (2oz), sifted
Raspberries 250g (9oz) (plus extra to serve)

For the raspberry coulis
Raspberries 225g (8oz)
Icing sugar 50g (2oz), sifted
Lemon juice 1 tsp

EQUIPMENT

Non-stick Swiss roll tin 33 x 28cm (13 x 11in)

Baking paper or kitchen foil

3 Gently fold in cornflour, vanilla extract and vinegar with a spatula or a metal spoon. Then scrape meringue onto prepared tin, spreading it up to the edges and levelling it as much as possible.
4 Cook for 45 mins–1 hour. Allow to cool in tin. Sprinkle a sheet of baking paper or kitchen foil with icing, or caster, sugar and turn out meringue onto it. Peel off backing paper or foil.

FILLING AND ROLLING

5 Whip cream until it forms soft peaks and then fold in vanilla and icing sugar. Spread it over meringue, leaving a

border of approximately 2.5cm (1in) around the edge.
6 Scatter raspberries evenly over cream and use sugared paper to help you roll up.

MAKING THE COULIS

7 Whizz raspberries in a blender or blitz briefly with a hand blender, push through a sieve and then stir in icing sugar and a little lemon juice.

SERVING

8 To serve, spoon some coulis onto each plate and then place a slice or two of roulade on top. Decorate with extra raspberries and sprigs of mint if you like.

Time: 1½ hrs	Serves 8	Fat 19g of which	V
	Calories 333	12g is saturated	

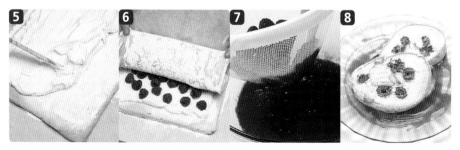

Perfect your technique
NAPOLEONS

For this variation on mille-feuille, the puff pastry is cooked to a biscuity crispness, layered with a scrumptious pastry cream and topped with icing.

"Draw horizontal chocolate lines at regular intervals "

These rich, delicate pastries demand really crisp pastry layers. So cook the sheets of pastry in a high-temperature oven and cover them during cooking with either a flat baking sheet or an appropriately sized baking tray. The idea is to weight the pastry into a compact layer as it cooks. Check towards the end of cooking time and remove the weight for the last few minutes so the pastry will have a golden finish. Allow the pastry sheets to cool completely. With the quantities shown, you will have one spare piece of cooked pastry to serve with fresh fruit and cream, if you like.

SECRETS OF PASTRY CREAM

Pastry cream or crème pâtissière is a thick custard sauce used in open fruit tarts and in many small pastry delicacies.

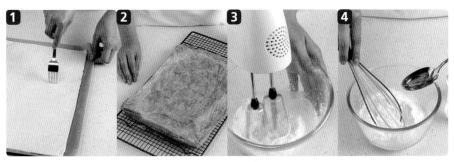

The recipe here uses cornflour to thicken the sauce; many recipes use custard powder instead. Both work well, but custard powder will give a yellow finish, whereas cornflour gives a cream-coloured result. Cook the sauce until it is really thick.

INGREDIENTS

For the pastry
Ready-rolled frozen puff pastry 2 x 375g packets, thawed

For the pastry cream
Egg yolks 3
Caster sugar 200g (7oz)
Plain flour 50g (2oz)
Cornflour 25g (1oz)

Milk 500ml (18fl oz)
Vanilla extract ½ tsp

For the glacé icing
Vanilla extract ¼ tsp
Icing sugar 225g (8oz), sifted

For the chocolate drizzle
Dark chocolate 25g (1oz)

EQUIPMENT

Baking sheets and/or trays
Baking paper

Cling film
Icing pen or piping bag

MAKING THE PASTRY LAYERS

1 Preheat oven to 220°C(200°fan)/425°F/Gas 7. Line 2 baking sheets with baking paper. Lay unrolled puff pastry sheets on prepared baking sheets, and prick them all over with a fork. Lay another baking sheet on top of each sheet of pastry. You may need to do this in batches.
2 Bake for 18–23 minutes, or until crisp and golden. Carefully remove pastry onto a rack to cool. Cut each sheet in half and trim edges. You will have one spare piece.

MAKING THE PASTRY CREAM

3 Beat egg yolks and sugar until white, add flour and cornflour and mix well. Add ¼ of milk to loosen mixture. Put remaining milk and vanilla extract into a pan and bring to boil. Pour onto eggs, stir well, return to heat and cook, stirring, until mixture thickens. Transfer to a bowl. Cover surface with cling film and cool completely without stirring.

MAKING THE GLACÉ ICING

4 Add vanilla extract to icing sugar and whisk in boiled water, spoon by spoon, until you get a good spreading consistency.

CREATING THE NAPOLEONS

5 Lay one sheet of cooked pastry onto a board and spread it with a thick layer of pastry cream. Lay a second sheet of pastry on top and spread on another layer of pastry cream.
6 Put on final layer of pastry and spread with an even layer of glacé icing.
7 Melt chocolate in a bowl over a pan of simmering water and put it into an icing pen or piping bag with a fine nozzle. Draw horizontal chocolate lines at regular intervals over surface of the icing.
8 Take a metal skewer and lightly drag it diagonally across lines to make an attractive pattern. Leave to set before slicing carefully with a sharp knife into individual servings.

| Time 1½ hrs | Makes 8-10 slices | Fat 18.3g of which | |
| | Calories 513 | 7.4g is saturated | |

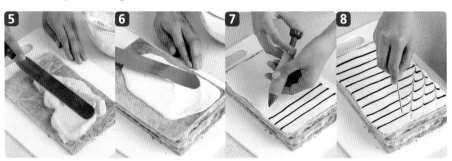

Stain REMOVAL

The most important factor in attacking stains is to act swiftly.
The newer the stain, whether greasy or non-greasy, or a combination
of the two, the easier it will be to remove without damage.

PERSONAL

Blood: Soak in biological detergent and cold water, or cold water with salt added, and wash in heavy-duty biological detergent. Or try rubbing a mixture of cornflour and cold water into the stain, leaving to dry and brushing off.

Collar and cuff dirt: Apply liquid biological detergent directly with an old toothbrush. Wash as usual.

Deodorant: Sponge with a hydrogen peroxide solution (see box); apply heavy-duty liquid detergent to the area; wash.

Perspiration: Dab with white vinegar solution (see box); leave for 5 minutes. Soak and wash in biological detergent.

SAFETY NOTE

Some of the cleaning agents you will need contain chemicals that are poisonous or flammable, so always read the label carefully and store them away from children. For safety, work in a well-ventilated area.

Urine and vomit: Soak in biological detergent and cold water, and wash in heavy-duty biological detergent.

FOODSTUFFS

Egg, milk and gravy: Soak in biological detergent and cold water, and wash in heavy-duty biological detergent.

Chewing gum: Freeze to make the gum brittle, using an ice cube inside a plastic bag; scrape it off, dab with methylated spirits (see box) and wash as usual.

Chocolate: Apply biological liquid detergent to the area; wash in heavy-duty detergent (containing bleach). On white items, soak in hydrogen peroxide solution (see box) and wash. Or soak in milk and wash in washing-up liquid; dab any remaining stain with white vinegar (see box), leave and wash as usual. Also good for coffee marks.

Oil/salad dressings: Sprinkle with cornflour to absorb grease, brush off, soak with washing-up liquid and then wash as normal.

BEVERAGES

Tea, coffee, soft drinks: Soak in cool water, use a pre-wash treatment and wash in heavy-duty detergent (with bleach). Or use a hydrogen peroxide solution (see box) before washing.

Red wine: Mop up excess liquid and treat as for oil. Or cover stain with salt and leave for 30 minutes. Sponge with a warm solution of biological detergent (with bleach), rinse with cold water and wash as normal. If the stain has dried, treat as for blood. On upholstery and carpets, blot with white kitchen paper. If it cannot be rinsed, spray with soda water, or white wine, then mop with kitchen paper.

White wine: Rinse with plenty of warm water, or treat as tea.

GREASE, GLUE, WAX, OIL AND TAR

Oil, fat, grease and tar: Dab the area with eucalyptus oil; wash in water as hot as the fabric allows.

Glue: Try to remove glue before it sets; apply methylated spirits (see box) for natural fabrics, or lighter fluid for synthetic fabrics.

Wax crayons, cosmetics and shoe polish: Treat with white spirit (see box) to remove the

CLEANING KIT

Detergents
Biological and heavy-duty liquid detergents.

Eucalyptus oil
Available from essential oils section of major chemists.

Hydrogen peroxide
Ask your chemist for 20 volume strength. Mix 1 part to 6 parts water; soak item for 30 minutes or until the stain has cleared.

Lighter fluid
Apply neat with cotton wool.

Methylated spirits
Available from diy stores. Apply with cotton-wool buds.

Pre-wash treatments
Some of these are formulated to treat a whole raft of common stains, some are more specific. Follow the instructions on the container.

White spirit
Dab neat on to grease stains.

White vinegar
Mix 15ml vinegar to 300ml water (3 tsp to ½ pint).

■ Chemical treatment may damage old or worn fabric.

■ Always test the fabric first in an inconspicuous area. If in doubt, take a stained garment to a dry-cleaner.

wax stain. Apply a pre-wash treatment and wash in heavy-duty detergent (with bleach).

MISCELLANEOUS

Grass and mud: Dab on methylated spirits (see box) and rinse off with warm soapy water. Apply a pre-wash treatment and then wash in heavy-duty detergent (with bleach). For a new stain, try soaking in white vinegar (see box), or squeeze on some lemon juice.

Ink, ballpoint and felt tip: Dab stain with methylated spirits, and then wash. For washable ink, soak in milk before laundering.

Mildew: Bleach white fabrics, or soak, then wash in heavy-duty detergent (with bleach).

Nail varnish: Mop up liquid, then with stain side facing down on kitchen paper, flush with nail polish remover (this is quite strong, and should not be used on some man-made fabrics – be sure to test first). Use methylated spirits (see box) to remove remaining nail-varnish colour.

Rust: Cover with salt, squeeze lemon juice over the salt and leave for about 1 hour; wash.

WHAT TO DO

■ Remove any solids with a blunt knife, and blot liquids with white kitchen paper.
■ Apply stain remover to a small, unseen area and wait 5–10 minutes. If the fabric reacts, seek dry-cleaning advice. Avoid treating delicate or expensive fabrics, or those that require dry-cleaning only.

■ Don't over-soak the fabric with a cleaning agent. To avoid making a ring mark, use a soft, absorbent cloth to apply the cleaning agent and work in a circular motion from the outside inwards. Dab, rather than rub, because rubbing can damage the fabric and it can also spread the stain.

Websites

diynot.com
persil.co.uk
stainexpert.co.uk

Washing SYMBOLS

Nearly all fabrics are machine washable these days, and most washing machines handle them with the care they deserve. Sort your clothes and linens by colour and fabric type, and check labels.

Unless absolutely necessary, try to wash clothes at 30 degrees, as this uses less energy and is kinder to the environment. It cuts down on bills, too. In any case, avoid washing an item at a higher temperature than recommended by the manufacturer, because this can cause it to shrink or the colour to run, which may affect other items in the load. Every so often, run a higher temperature programme with the machine empty, to clean out greasy residues and kill off any bacteria.

LOADING TIPS

■ Fill your washing machine loosely. Overloading not only adds to the number of creases that will need ironing out, but can damage your clothes and even your machine.
■ If you are washing woollens, this may mean washing just two or three items in one load.

TEXTILE CYCLES

Check both the temperature, given by the figure in the tub, and the machine-action bar(s) under it. The temperature may be indicated by dots (six for 95°, four for 60°, two for 40° and one for 30°).

 Maximum agitation. Cotton cycle
White cotton or linen articles without special finishes.

 Maximum agitation. Cotton cycle
Cotton, linen or viscose articles without special finishes where colours are fast at 60°C.

 Maximum agitation. Cotton cycle
Cotton, linen or viscose where colours are fast at 40°C but not at 60°C.

 Medium agitation. Synthetic cycle
Acrylics, acetate or triacetate, including mixtures with wool, polyester and wool blends.

 Minimum agitation. Wool cycle
Wool, including blankets, wool mixed with other fibres, and silk.

 Gentle agitation. Delicates cycle
Silk, acetates and mixed synthetics not colourfast at 40°C.

 HAND WASH ONLY
See garment label for further instructions.

 DO NOT MACHINE OR HAND WASH

WASHING PROCESS

Garments with labels showing the wash tub without the bar may be mixed with those that do, provided that they are washed at the lowest temperature shown and the gentlest setting of machine agitation to protect delicate items.

 NO BAR
Normal – maximum machine action

 1 BAR
Medium – reduced machine action

 2 BARS
Minimum – lowest machine action

DRY-CLEANING/BLEACHING

A circle shows the item may be dry-cleaned and the letter P or F indicates the cleaning fluids that may be used by your professional dry-cleaner.

 May be dry-cleaned

 Do not dry-clean

 Bleach may be used

 Do not use chlorine bleach

 Do not bleach

WASHING SYMBOLS

 WASH TUB: Washing process

 TRIANGLE: Bleaching

 IRON: Ironing settings

 SQUARE: Drying methods

 CIRCLE: Dry cleaning

DRYING SYMBOLS

Check the label to see if your garment can be tumble-dried; the label may advise using a reduced heat setting by putting a single dot within the circle. Two dots indicate a higher heat setting.

 May be tumble-dried

 Do not tumble-dry

 Hang dry

 Drip dry recommended

 Dry flat

IRONING

■ The dots inside the iron indicate the temperature setting. One dot represents the coolest setting and three dots are for the hottest temperature. The table (right) is a guide to the temperature to use for specific types of fabric.
■ You should always use the setting recommended by the manufacturer. For some materials the advice may be that you iron on the wrong side of the fabric only, so check the label.
■ To avoid creases, store your clothes in drawers and wardrobes loosely; don't pack them in.

 HOT (3 DOTS) Cotton, linen and viscose fabrics.

 WARM (2 DOTS)
Polyester mixtures and wool.

COOL (1 DOT) Acrylic, nylon, acetate, triacetate and polyester.

DO NOT IRON

Mastering the WEB

Whether you choose a laptop, tablet or smartphone, your electronic device will not only keep you in touch with family and friends, it will also keep you entertained and informed wherever you are. Speedy, easy, convenient – what's not to like?

When British computer scientist Tim Berners-Lee introduced mankind to the World Wide Web, did he have any idea of the scale of his invention? Maybe he did know that the technology he was unleashing was world-changing, but as the realisation dawned on the rest of us, mostly we were simply flabbergasted!

For anyone who hasn't grown up with computer technology, the whole idea is still pretty much mind-blowing. But although the science may be impossible to grasp, unless you happen to be a physicist, the point is you don't have to understand it. It's not necessary to know how it all works, just how to use it. While some people may be able to carry on in their own internet-free world, for most of us that's impossible since just about everything depends on computers these days. In the end, there's really no option but to welcome the technology into our lives and use it to our advantage, and there's no denying that the speed, convenience and informative nature of the online system can make life a lot easier.

WHAT TO CHOOSE?

The next question is how to join the computer-savvy crowd, and that's often a stumbling block. Laptop, tablet, smartphone? They all allow you to email, join social media, watch films and videos, read a book, listen to music, shop, play games and search for information on the internet, among many other things. You just need to know the right keys to press! So your own choice of electronic device or devices depends on what you want to use it for.

Laptops: many people have them to use at home as a less cumbersome, and movable, alternative to a full-sized desktop computer. Laptops have decent-sized screens and a proper keyboard, making it easier to browse the internet, view photographs, fill in online forms and type long emails or other documents. They also have plenty of storage space, and several sockets (USB ports) for connecting to a printer, TV, digital camera or other devices.

Tablets: the Apple iPad and iPad mini are tablets, as is Kindle Fire and other brands that use the Android or Windows operating systems. They are light, slim and easily carried, and have a bigger screen than smartphones (but smaller than laptops). Tablets are great

travelling companions because not only are they good for entertainment on the move, they also take photographs. The touchscreen keyboard is fine for short emails, once you get used to it, and tablets have a longer battery life than either laptops or smartphones.

Smartphones: these are mobile phones that do everything tablets and laptops do, and you can carry them in your pocket. The main difference is that the screens are smaller, so they are not the best for watching films. Most do not offer a proper keyboard either and so typing can be laborious.

SOCIAL MEDIA

There are hundreds of social media sites, some for general chat, including Facebook, Twitter and YouTube, and some with a more specialised slant, such as Instagram, which is all about sharing images. Even if you don't want to participate, they can be a useful source of information on subjects that you're interested in, and can be a great way of linking up with old friends.

DAIRY DIARY

You can find just about anything that you need or like online - even the Dairy Diary! Read the weekly blog with its enticing recipes, garden ideas, crafts and family fun. Browse the website for exciting competitions, a comprehensive recipe library and fascinating features. You can even purchase your diary and fabulous cookbooks. Be the first to hear about news and giveaways via Facebook and Twitter as well as enjoying the daily hints and tips. On Facebook you can even post your own comments and converse with fellow Dairy Diary fans.

"The informative nature of the online system can make life a lot easier"

"We breathe in oxygen and breathe out carbon dioxide; trees do the opposite"

Grow your own TREE

Trees, beautiful and ever-changing, bring a reassuring sense of continuity – plant a tree and in the normal course of events it will be there for generations to come. Besides this, the bare fact is that trees play a vital role in all our lives.

We breathe in oxygen and breathe out carbon dioxide; trees do the opposite, although in fact they store carbon dioxide rather than releasing this 'greenhouse gas' into the atmosphere. The leaves absorb various pollutants including nitrous oxides, sulphur dioxide and carbon monoxide. So trees not only produce oxygen but help clean the air, too, and they help to decontaminate the soil by absorbing noxious chemicals, either storing them or changing them into a less harmful state. These are the fundamental reasons why it is so important to maintain woodlands and parks, especially in urban areas.

There's more: trees prevent soil erosion, slow down water run-off (particularly important in storm or flood conditions), act as windbreaks, deaden noise and give shade and shelter. They provide natural habitats for birds, insects and other animals, support other plant life and offer a terrific harvest in the form of timber, fruit and nuts, not to mention soil-enriching compost from leaf fall. Life would be poorer – not to say impossible – without trees, so the more of them the better.

At least two charities are on the case. The Woodland Trust organises tree planting, including acres of new woodland to commemorate the First World War, as does the Tree Council, which also runs National Tree Week as an annual autumn event (check websites for details). The National Trust is another great defender and planter of trees.

A ONE-OFF

On a less ambitious scale, you could consider cultivating your own tree. Just one would be a great asset to the garden whether deciduous or evergreen.

ANCIENT TREE HUNT

Some trees have been around for so long it's hard to appreciate just how incredibly old they are, especially yews. The Fortingall Yew in Perthshire is thought to be 5000 years old, the oldest tree in Europe. The Borrowdale Yews, near Seathwaite in Cumbria, inspired Wordsworth to write his poem 'Yew-Trees' and are thought to be 2000 years old. Oaks, limes, planes and sweet chestnuts are among other extremely long livers. The Woodland Trust is compiling a database of these magnificent specimens, calling the project the Ancient Tree Hunt, and you can take part. Whenever you're out in woods or parks, or passing an old cemetery, keep an eye out for these venerable relics – they are likely to have a huge girth and a gnarled, well-weathered look. Note approximate measurements and location, take photos if you can and report back to the Woodland Trust (check website for details).

PRACTICALITIES

It can be worrying if you have a tree near the house, but usually it's not a problem – as far away from the house as it's tall is a good rule of thumb, and keep it neat and well pruned. It may be a good idea to have it surveyed from time to time, so that if any problems do arise, they can be nipped in the bud.

Serious subsidence or structural damage to a building are rarely the fault of a tree, although it may add to the problem; and subsidence may be a risk on clay in prolonged dry weather, since the tree taking water from the soil may cause shrinkage. Generally, tree roots don't block drains – only if the drain is already damaged, allowing the roots a way in.

A tree is the responsibility of the landowner, and so you may be liable for any damage caused by branches breaking off in the wind, for example. Check your insurance to make sure you're covered, and for specific conditions that may apply to your property. And before doing anything drastic to a tree, check with the Local Authority to see whether it's subject to a Tree Preservation Order (when various restrictions apply).

PLANTING A TREE

Autumn and winter are the recommended times to plant a tree, whether bare-rooted or container grown. About a month beforehand, prepare the site by loosening the soil and digging in some organic matter or fertiliser. in a wide area (about 3m/10ft).

When it comes to planting, leave the tree in a bucket of water for an hour, still in its pot, if that's how it came. Dig the hole as deep as the roots and about three times as wide. The base of the trunk should be a fraction above the soil when the hole is backfilled.

Backfilling is a job for two. Ask someone to hold the tree upright and make sure soil fills in around the roots, leaving no air pockets – best done with your hands. Firm the soil, not too hard. No need for more fertiliser, which may damage fragile roots, but do mulch with well-rotted compost, not right up to the stem. Support the sapling with a stake or two, secured with tree ties. Remember to loosen them as the tree grows.

The young tree will need plenty of watering in its first few years (even if it rains a lot!) and it's best to keep the area around it clear of other plants. Mulching is good but, again, not right up to the trunk because if this is constantly damp, the bark may rot.

" Consider how tall your tree is likely to grow and how much it will spread "

Think about whether you want one that produces lovely flowers in the spring, such as a magnolia, or has colourful foliage in the autumn, such as a maple. A fruit tree will provide you with a succulent harvest or perhaps you prefer a tree that's purely decorative, such an ornamental cherry, paperbark maple or a weeping silver pear.

Consider how tall your tree is likely to grow and how much it will spread. When deciding where to put it, and whether you want it to be a focal point in the garden, take into account how the shade cast will affect the house and the rest of the garden, and indeed your neighbour's house and garden.

Soil type is critical. Different species of tree prefer different conditions, so don't skimp on your research. Get the match wrong and your long-term beauty is likely to turn into a short-term flop. You can grow a small tree in a container, and thus control soil type, but position the container carefully because, once your tree starts growing, the pot may be difficult to move.

Websites

forestry.gov.uk
nationaltrust.org.uk
rhs.org.uk
treecouncil.org.uk
woodlandtrust.org.uk

"Walking is one of the most enjoyable ways of improving your health "

Walking for HEALTH

Many of us don't give it a thought – putting one foot in front of the other is second nature – but, in fact, walking is one of the most healthful activities you can undertake, and not only does it bring physical benefits, it makes you feel better, too.

No matter your age or level of fitness, walking is one of the easiest, and most enjoyable, ways of improving your health, and it can be as gentle or challenging as you wish. Even a short stroll will exercise a few muscles, burn a few calories and release a few endorphins. These are the feel-good hormones that circulate when you take any physical exercise, and enhance your sense of wellbeing. A dose of endorphins can leave you feeling more energetic, more cheerful and certainly less tired than if you'd spent that half an hour slumped on the sofa in front of the TV (tempting as that may be).

Keeping up a brisk pace for a mile (which takes around 20 minutes) burns 100+ calories – of course, you burn more stored fat if you walk faster or farther (and even more if you do both). Optimum pace varies from person to person. A good general guideline is that it should be fast enough to make you breathe a bit harder than usual without actually panting or getting a stitch. You should still be able to hold a conversation without gasping for breath.

So walking helps you to control your weight and has a positive effect on your stress levels. When it comes to reducing stress, aside from generating endorphins, walking scores in lowering the irritation factor – it's much less frustrating than coping with late/infrequent trains or buses, or traffic jams. What else? It also helps combat heart disease, breast cancer, colon cancer, type 2 diabetes and stroke; and strengthening leg muscles and hamstrings helps to protect hip and knee joints.

The NHS is keen for us to take 10,000 steps each and every day (up from the average 3–4,000). Most medical authorities agree that we should aim for 150 minutes of moderate-intensity aerobic activity per week, i.e. something to get the heart beating faster and maybe induce a light sweat, such as brisk walking. Fortunately, it doesn't have to be all at once; you can do it in bouts as short as ten minutes. But the consensus is plain – walking is good for you.

45

GETTING STARTED

If you haven't done much exercise for a while, walking is a good way to get back into it. The best advice is to start slowly and gradually build up speed and distance – walk to the shops, take a walk at lunchtime, get off a stop early, walk to meet a friend. Of course, if you have a dog, you have a head start. Just take it for longer walks more often. If boredom's your worry, try listening to music, or go in company. If you can't persuade friends or family to come along regularly, join a local walking group or the Ramblers.

Filling your lungs with fresh sea or country air is great motivation for getting out and about, but exploring the city streets can be just as much fun. You can combine it with sight-seeing, visiting historic sites and discovering places you never knew about before.

Once you're in the swing, you could try some longer walks. The right kit and good posture will help avoid excessive aches and pains. Neck and shoulders should be relaxed but not rounded, hunched or slumped, and arms and shoulders should swing naturally, which exercises

your side muscles. Do a few gentle stretches afterwards, concentrating on hamstrings, quadriceps and calves, to avoid any stiffening up – do them beforehand, too, if you're going off on a trek.

If you like the idea of one of the many long-distance routes that abound throughout the country but are daunted by the prospect of such an ambitious walk, bear in mind that you don't have to do the whole trail; you can go for a day's walk or do a few miles (or less) if you like. Just do whatever suits you. Pick your section of the trail and enjoy it.

KIT

Technical advances in the design of outdoor clothes and their materials carry on apace. If you're planning anything more ambitious than an evening stroll after dinner, go to one of the many specialist outdoors shops or websites and garner some advice on what to wear and what to take with you.

■ The main item you need is a pair of good, comfortable shoes that don't squash your toes and have a cushioned sole that's not rigid, so your foot can roll from heel to toe – hit the ground with the heel, push off with the toes. Trainers are fine for shorter walks, but if you get hooked and decide to take on a few longer treks, you'd be better off with designated walking shoes or boots. Proper walking socks are also a good defence against blisters.

■ Loose, comfortable clothes are ideal, preferably in a

sweat-wicking fabric. Bear in mind that walking in denim can be uncomfortable. Try wearing layers on top, rather than one item that's thick and heavy.

■ An inexpensive pedometer will help you to keep track of how far you're going (good if you're keen to achieve the 10,000 steps per day as recommended by the NHS).

■ If you're going to be out hiking all day, or even for a few hours, you'll need to take some provisions: water, energy bars/food, map or guidebook, first-aid kit, extra top, rain gear and possibly sunscreen, sunglasses and sunhat. It's best not to go alone and to tell someone where you're going – and don't forget your mobile phone.

NATIONAL TRAILS

There are 15 National Trails, long-distance walking routes through some of the most awe-inspiring scenery in England and Wales (the equivalent north of the border is Scotland's Great Trails). Some sections are fairly gentle, some challenging; all are rewarding. From the South Downs Way and the Ridgeway to Hadrian's Wall Path and the Pennine Way, the trails are there for you to enjoy. England's Coast Path, a new National Trail, will eventually take you around the English coast, all 2,755 miles (4,500km) of it. Some sections are open (see website for details), and when it's completed, it will be one of the longest coastal walking paths in the world.

WALKING BY WATER

If you're looking for a quiet time, head for the towpath, and open up to the soporific effect of water and nature. It doesn't matter how long you've got – even a short stroll can do you

" Keeping up a brisk pace for a mile burns 100+ calories "

good, and some great long-distance footpaths wind along beside rivers and canals. You can walk from the source of the River Wye to the sea, if you've a mind (138 miles/222km), or follow Shakespeare's Avon Way (88 miles/142km), and the Derby Canal Ring (28 miles/45km) takes you beside several canals back to where you started. Check the Inland Waterways Association and the Long Distance Walkers Association websites for suggestions and information.

TAKE TO THE HILLS

Hill walking undoubtedly has a romantic ring to it but it needs proper planning. Try a gentle hill first, and have a break at the top. If you find it's for you, and your fitness allows, plan a route and take advice from experienced walkers. Be careful not to overdo it – the walking plan is supposed

to prevent heart attacks, not cause them! If you're worried about how walking (or any exercise regime) may effect existing health problems, consult your GP.

If you take to hill walking like grouse to heather, Wainwright's coast to coast across northern England (192 miles/309km) may be something to aim for. The John Muir Way (134 miles/215km) runs coast to coast across central Scotland and has hilly sections.

Websites

nationaltrail.co.uk
nhs.uk
ramblers.org.uk
walk4life.info
walkengland.org.uk
(now called Walk Unlimited)
walkhighlands.co.uk
walkswithbuggies.com
waterways.org.uk

Inland WATERWAYS

A day spent exploring the pleasures an inland waterway has to offer is fun for everyone, doers and idlers alike. It's a wonderful way to recharge the batteries, and you don't have to take to the water – the towpath is a fantastic public amenity.

ritain is shot through with inland waterways – some 2,000 miles of canals and navigable rivers flow through our towns, villages and countryside, and chances are you live within fairly easy reach of one of them. In this busy world, if you feel the need to switch off and take a few hours' relaxation, or for a different family day out, why not let the waterway work its magic?

" *Our inland waterways are undergoing a renaissance* "

HERITAGE

Man-made structures, essential to keep the waterways working, are well to the fore. Many of them are evidence of an innovative industrial past and represent engineering breakthroughs, including aqueducts, locks, bridges and tunnels. The Standedge tunnel, which takes the Huddersfield Canal beneath the Pennines, is the longest in Britain at 16,499ft (5,029m). You can take a boat trip along it, or, if enclosed spaces are not for you, linger in the pub or visitor centre and hear about it from the rest of the day-outers.

Nowadays, our inland waterways are undergoing a renaissance as a means of leisure and recreation, but their original purpose, in the absence of substantial road and rail networks, was as a means of freight transport. The Bridgewater Canal is usually regarded as the one that started the rush of canal building in the 18th century. It was the brainchild of the Duke of Bridgewater, inspired by a visit to the Canal du Midi in France. His mines in Worsley supplied coal to Manchester and once the canal was finished, in 1776, the price of coal in that city practically halved. Others took note and more canals were built, especially in the north and midlands where heavy industries were king and goods needed to be transported to cities and ports as cheaply as possible.

Interestingly, canals were not financed by the government but by industrialists, mine and mill owners, textile manufacturers and banks, and each one required an Act of Parliament to enable it to go ahead.

LOCKS

These are synonymous with canals. Mostly they are widely spaced and often you'll find an attractive keeper's cottage beside them, or a charming waterside pub, where you can sit and watch the boats to your heart's content.

Lock gates are always intriguing, whether the vertical, lifting type or mitre gates. Lifting gates originated in China in the 10th century while the idea for mitre gates – those held together in a V-shape by water pressure – is usually credited to Leonardo da Vinci, artist and inventor, who designed a version of them for the San Marco lock in Milan at the end of the 15th century.

Several canals have a spectacular series of locks, known as flights. The Kennet and Avon, for instance, has 29 (the Caen Hill Locks). Sixteen of them rise in a steep line up the hillside with hardly a couple of boat lengths between them. They enable the canal to rise 237ft (72m) in just 2 miles and are a surprising sight, but this is not the longest flight of locks in Britain. That accolade goes to the Tardebigge flight – 30 narrow locks on the Worcester and Birmingham Canal, which

raise the waterway some 220ft (67m) in 2¼ miles. The Hatton flight on the Grand Union Canal near Warwick is another worth a visit – 21 locks in 2 miles, hard work for boaters, fun for walkers.

BOAT LIFTS

In Anderton in Cheshire, the River Weaver and the Trent and Mersey Canal were separated by a vertical drop of 50ft (over 15m). How to connect them? A boat lift was the answer and so in 1875, they built one. Boats rested in water-filled troughs and were hydraulically lifted from river to canal and vice versa. This amazing feat of Victorian engineering remained in use until 1983 when corrosion got the better of it. However, it has been lovingly restored, re-opened in 2002 and is now a Scheduled Monument.

Right at the other end of the spectrum is the Falkirk Wheel, the only other boat lift in Britain. Opened in 2002, this futuristic rotating lift raises boats 79ft (24m) from the Forth and Clyde Canal to the Union Canal. At the top, boats have to negotiate an aqueduct and two locks to reach the canal. Boat trips are, understandably, hugely popular and there is a visitor centre.

MUSEUMS

■ National Waterways Museum, Ellesmere Port
■ Gloucester Waterways Museum
■ Stoke Bruerne Canal Museum, Towcester, Northants.

The Heritage Boatyard, part of the National Waterways Museum, trains young people in traditional skills that might otherwise be lost. It's part funded by the Boat Museum Society, an organisation that aims to preserve historic boats together with the skills, knowledge and way of life of the waterways.

TOWPATHS

An intrinsic part of a visit to a waterway is, of course, the towpath, a flat walkway ideal for strolling, jogging, playing with the kids, cycling, angling, nature watching, people watching – whatever takes your fancy. The waterways have become a haven for wildlife, from mallard and moorhens to kingfishers and herons. If you're lucky you may even see an otter or water vole, and all for free (although you need a licence to fish). Boat trips are often available, and how delightful to float along at a snail's pace, idly watching the world go by. If you have the necessary skill, you could hire a boat, but you need a licence to use your own, including a canoe.

CHARITIES

In England and Wales, the charitable Canal and River Trust took over from the government-owned British Waterways in 2012 as the organisation responsible for the waterways, structures, docks and surrounding landscape. In Scotland, responsibility remains with a public corporation, Scottish Canals.

The Inland Waterways Association, founded in 1946, continues to campaign for the use, maintenance and restoration of Britain's inland waterways. IWA's interests include boating, towpath walking, industrial archaeology, nature conservation and many other activities associated with the inland waterways, and they encourage children to participate with their Wild Over Waterways (WoW) section.

Both organisations are always looking for volunteers, so if you discover a love for the waterways, want to help preserve them and have some spare time, why not lend a hand?

Websites

boatmuseumsociety.org.uk
canalrivertrust.org.uk
waterways.org.uk

AQUEDUCTS

These were among the most ambitious solutions to the problem of achieving the most direct route possible from mine or factory to town or port. Aqueducts are still in use on several canals, occasionally with towpaths, although in some cases you may need a good head for heights to stroll along them. Here is a selection:

Pontcysyllte: at 1,007ft (307m) long and 126ft (38m) high, Thomas Telford's aqueduct is the longest and highest in the UK. It carries the Llangollen Canal over the River Dee in Wrexham, and was completed in 1805, having taken ten years to build. In 2009 it was made a World Heritage site.
Edstone: this early 19th-century, cast-iron aqueduct is the longest in England at 475ft (145m). It carries a section of the Stratford-upon-Avon Canal in Warwickshire.
Avon: Scotland's longest and highest aqueduct is no longer operational. Once it carried the Union Canal; now it runs through the Muiravonside Country Park, near Linlithgow, and you can walk across to see spectacular views.
Lune: built in classical style, this aqueduct carries canal and towpath over the River Lune in Lancaster. Originally completed in 1796 at vast expense, it has had a £2 million renovation.
Barton Swing: literally, a swing bridge carrying a canal! It swings 90° to allow traffic to pass along the Manchester Ship Canal, then swings back again to allow narrow boats to carry on along the Bridgewater Canal. Opened in 1894. Amazing!

Quirky places to STAY

Hotels are fine and B&Bs great, but what about staying in a converted chapel, a lighthouse or a windmill? It's not too difficult to find a venue offbeat enough to satisfy the wildest craving for the curious, fanciful or downright eccentric.

Many of us are tempted by the idea of spending a few days somewhere a bit different, and accommodation plays a big part in our choice. From apartments in stately homes to youth hostels in castles, enticingly odd places to spend your precious leisure time have never been so varied. And if self-catering holds no appeal, there are plenty of themed hotels around to cater for your every need, such as the kitsch La Rosa in Whitby, the Enchanted Manor on the Isle of Wight or The Joker, a Batman barge on Merseyside.

Often, the quirkiest places to stay are those that have been converted from their original purpose. In North Yorkshire, for instance, you can bed down in an extremely grand pigsty, built over a hundred years ago by the squire of Fyling Hall to resemble a Greek temple. As you gaze across the hills from the columned portico towards Robin Hood's Bay, you can only wonder at the good squire's motivation.

Windmills and watermills are also high on the list of conversions, along with water towers. The Appleton Water Tower, on the edge of the Sandringham estate in Norfolk, is an octagonal Victorian edifice that commands great views from the top, while the House in the Clouds in Thorpeness has to be seen to be believed – a cottage, which was the water tank,

perched on top of a wooden-cladded, many-windowed tower, which now provides five floors of comfortable accommodation.

Besides lighthouses, seaside structures that lend themselves to conversion include martello towers. The one at Aldeburgh in Suffolk was built as a defence against Napoleon's forces, and is actually four towers fused into one building. It stands defiantly right on the shingle beach – heaven for anyone who loves the sea, whatever the weather.

Former schoolhouses, chapels, banks and jails are just a few of the other rum places you could choose to rest your weary head.

CLOSE TO NATURE

For those who remain big kids at heart, a treehouse is irresistible. Being hugged by the branches of an aged oak is exciting for youngsters and as therapeutic as it gets for everyone else. Any number are available to rent in woodlands and country estates around the land – just pray the wind gods are kind.

If you like the idea of camping but baulk at the practicalities, why not try a yurt? These grand tents are springing up like Mongolian mushrooms and the

" For those who remain big kids at heart, a treehouse is irresistible "

TRANSPORT-BASED LETS

Old-fashioned ways of getting from A to B seem to be favourites for refurbishing as holiday lets. Converted railway carriages galore are scattered around the country, waiting to charm old railway buffs and delight new ones. Disused stations are also prime candidates for the change of use category, along with buses, especially double-deckers, and airstream retro trailers. If you want to hit the road in your holiday home, classic VW campervans are a good bet and quite easy to rent.

reality of this kind of camping is a lot more luxurious than you may remember from the Guides and Scouts. Teepees also offer more comfort than the average experience under canvas, while shepherd's huts or bothies located on quiet hillsides provide a great retreat from civilisation (with or without all mod cons!)

Websites

canopyandstars.co.uk
historic-uk.com
landmarktrust.org.uk
nationaltrust.org.uk
oneoffplaces.co.uk
quirkyaccom.co.uk
statelyhomes.com
sykescottages.co.uk
visitbritain.com
windmillworld.com

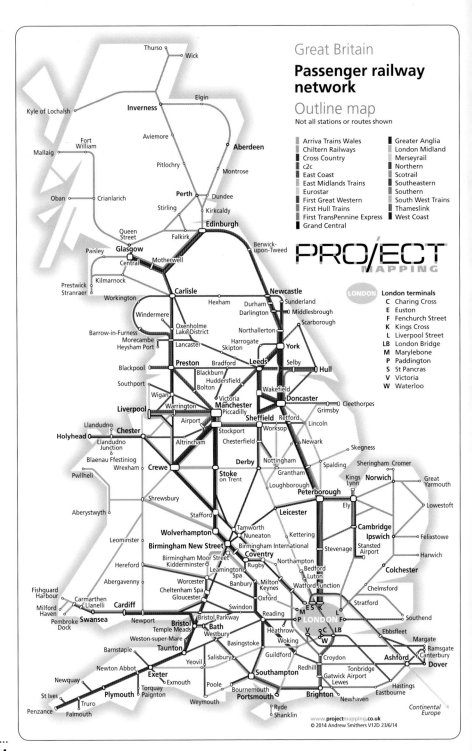

Great Britain

Passenger railway network

Outline map
Not all stations or routes shown

Arriva Trains Wales	Greater Anglia
Chiltern Railways	London Midland
Cross Country	Merseyrail
c2c	Northern
East Coast	Scotrail
East Midlands Trains	Southeastern
Eurostar	Southern
First Great Western	South West Trains
First Hull Trains	Thameslink
First TransPennine Express	West Coast
Grand Central	

PRO/ECT
MAPPING

LONDON

London terminals
C	Charing Cross
E	Euston
F	Fenchurch Street
K	Kings Cross
L	Liverpool Street
LB	London Bridge
M	Marylebone
P	Paddington
S	St Pancras
V	Victoria
W	Waterloo

www.projectmapping.co.uk
© 2014 Andrew Smithers V12D 23/6/14

Dɑiry
Diɑry
2016

December

M	T	W	T	F	S	S	M	T	W	T	F	S	S
21	22	23	24	25	26	27	**28**	**29**	**30**	**31**	**1**	**2**	**3**

28 Monday

29 Tuesday

30 Wednesday

31 Thursday

New Year's Eve

1 Friday JANUARY

New Year's Day
Bank Holiday, UK

M	T	W	T	F	S	S	M	T	W	T	F	S	S
4	5	6	7	8	9	10	11	12	13	14	15	16	17

January
Week 53

Saturday 2
(*Last Quarter*

Sunday 3

Goat's Cheese & Red Onion Tarts

Ready-rolled puff pastry
175g (6oz)
Butter 25g (1oz)
Olive oil 2 tbsp
Red onions 2 large, peeled and
thinly sliced
Caster sugar ½ tsp
Goat's cheese 2 x 100g (3½oz)
rounds, halved
Wild rocket 25g (1oz)

1 Cut pastry into four 10cm
(4in) circles (flute with finger,
thumb and a small knife for a
decorative effect). Place on a
baking sheet and chill.
2 Heat butter and oil in a
saucepan until foaming. Add
onions and sugar and cook
gently for 15-20 minutes until
softened, stirring often.
3 Season to taste and leave to
cool for 10 minutes.
4 Preheat oven to
220°C(200°fan)/425°F/Gas 7.
Divide onions between circles,
keeping 1cm (½in) in from rim.
Set cheese on top and push
down gently to nestle amongst
onions. Bake for 15-20 minutes
until pastry is puffed and golden.

5 Top with rocket and serve.
(Leftover pastry can be frozen or
made into cheese straws.)

Time 50 mins plus cooling	**Serves** 4 **Calories** 451	**Fat** 34g of which 18g is saturated	V F

January

M	T	W	T	F	S	S	M	T	W	T	F	S	S
28	29	30	31	1	2	3	4	5	6	7	8	9	10

4 Monday

Bank Holiday, Scotland

5 Tuesday

6 Wednesday

Epiphany

7 Thursday

8 Friday

M	T	W	T	F	S	S	M	T	W	T	F	S	S
11	12	13	14	15	16	17	18	19	20	21	22	23	24

January
Week 1

Saturday **9**

Sunday **10**

● *New Moon*

Sweet Chilli Stir-Fried Pork

Sunflower oil 1 tbsp
Boneless pork loin steaks
2, fat removed and thinly sliced
Stir-fry vegetables 220g pack
Straight-to-wok noodles
350g pack
Toasted sesame oil 1 tbsp
Sweet chilli dipping sauce
2-3 tbsp

1 Heat oil in a wok or non-stick frying pan until very hot, add pork strips and stir-fry for about 3 minutes.
2 Add vegetables and continue stir-frying for another 2-3 minutes.
3 Add noodles with sesame oil and chilli sauce and heat through until everything is cooked and hot.

Time 15 mins	**Serves** 2	**Fat** 17g of which
	Calories 540	2.8g is saturated

January

M	T	W	T	F	S	S	M	T	W	T	F	S	S
4	5	6	7	8	9	10	11	12	13	14	15	16	17

11 Monday

12 Tuesday

13 Wednesday

14 Thursday

15 Friday

M	T	W	T	F	S	S	M	T	W	T	F	S	S
18	19	20	21	22	23	24	25	26	27	28	29	30	31

January
Week 2

Saturday 16

❭ *First Quarter*

Sunday 17

Notes

January

M	T	W	T	F	S	S	M	T	W	T	F	S	S
11	12	13	14	15	16	17	**18**	19	20	21	22	23	24

18 Monday

19 Tuesday

20 Wednesday

21 Thursday

22 Friday

M	T	W	T	F	S	S	M	T	W	T	F	S	S
25	26	27	28	29	30	31	1	2	3	4	5	6	7

January
Week 3

Saturday 23

Sunday 24

○ *Full Moon*
Septuagesima Sunday

Gingered Beef Casserole

Sunflower oil 1 tbsp
Diced stewing beef 500g
(1lb 2oz)
Onion 1, peeled and chopped
Plain flour 1 tbsp
Ginger beer 500ml (18fl oz)
Beef stock 300ml (½ pint)
Worcestershire sauce 1 tbsp
English mustard 1 tsp
Carrots 350g (12oz), peeled,
halved lengthways, thickly sliced
Pearl barley 110g (4oz)

1 Preheat oven to
180°C(160°fan)/350°F/Gas 4.
Heat oil in a large frying pan,
add beef and fry, stirring, for
3 minutes. Add onion and fry,
stirring, until meat is browned
and onion has softened.
2 Stir in flour then gradually mix
in ginger beer and stock. Add
Worcestershire sauce, mustard,
carrots and barley, then season.
Bring up to boil, stirring.
3 Transfer to an ovenproof
casserole dish, cover and bake
for 2 hours until meat is tender.

Time 2½ hrs   **Serves** 4   **Fat** 21g of which
Calories 416   4g is saturated

63

January

M	T	W	T	F	S	S	M	T	W	T	F	S	S
18	19	20	21	22	23	24	25	26	27	28	29	30	31

25 Monday

Burns' Night

26 Tuesday

27 Wednesday

28 Thursday

29 Friday

M	T	W	T	F	S	S	M	T	W	T	F	S	S
1	2	3	4	5	6	7	8	9	10	11	12	13	14

January
Week 4

Saturday **30**

Sunday **31**

Westmorland Pepper Cake

Butter 75g (3oz)
Raisins 75g (3oz)
Currants 75g (3oz)
Caster sugar 110g (4oz)
Self-raising flour 225g (8oz)
Ground ginger ½ tsp
Ground cloves ½ tsp
Finely ground black pepper
½ tsp
Milk 4 tbsp
Egg 1, beaten
Lancashire cheese to serve,
optional

1 Preheat oven to
180°C(160°fan)/350°F/Gas 4.
Grease and line a deep 18cm
(7in) round cake tin.
2 Put butter, fruit, sugar and
150ml (¼ pint) water in a
saucepan and bring up to boil.
Simmer for 10 minutes and then
leave to cool for 10 minutes.
3 In a bowl mix together flour,
spices and pepper. Stir in fruit,
milk and egg. Pour into tin.
4 Bake for 45 minutes, until firm
and golden. Cool on a wire rack.

| **Time** 1 hr plus cooling | **Makes** 12 slices **Calories** 187 | **Fat** 6g of which 3.5g is saturated | V F |

February

M	T	W	T	F	S	S	M	T	W	T	F	S	S
25	26	27	28	29	30	31	1	2	3	4	5	6	7

1 Monday FEBRUARY

☾ *Last Quarter*

2 Tuesday

3 Wednesday

4 Thursday

5 Friday

M	T	W	T	F	S	S	M	T	W	T	F	S	S
8	9	10	11	12	13	14	15	16	17	18	19	20	21

February
Week 5

Saturday 6
Accession of Queen Elizabeth II

Sunday 7
Quinquagesima Sunday

Garlic Roast Poussin

Potatoes 2 large, peeled and cut into chunks
Olive oil 3 tbsp
Garlic 2 cloves, peeled and chopped
Poussin 2, preferably corn fed
Fresh tarragon 2 sprigs
Back bacon 2 rashers, halved lengthways
Prepared leeks, peas and spinach 200g packet, to serve

1 Preheat oven to 200°C(180°fan)/400°F/Gas 6. Cook potatoes in a saucepan of simmering water for 5 minutes. Drain, then shake to rough up the edges.
2 Meanwhile, heat 2 tbsp oil in a large roasting tin in the oven for 5 minutes.
3 Mix remaining oil with garlic and brush over poussin. Set a tarragon sprig on top and criss cross with bacon.
4 Carefully add potatoes to hot oil in roasting tin, baste and push to side of tin.

Time 1½ hrs	Serves 2	Fat 54g of which
	Calories 935	10.7g is saturated

5 Place poussin in centre of tin, season and baste, then roast for 25 minutes. Baste poussin again then roast for 20-25 minutes more until cooked.

6 Cook vegetables according to packet's instructions. Serve with poussin, potatoes and juices from tin. If poussin is unavailable use chicken (extra roasting time).

February

M	T	W	T	F	S	S	M	T	W	T	F	S	S
1	2	3	4	5	6	7	8	9	10	11	12	13	14

8 Monday

● *New Moon*

9 Tuesday

Shrove Tuesday

10 Wednesday

Ash Wednesday

11 Thursday

12 Friday

M	T	W	T	F	S	S	M	T	W	T	F	S	S
15	16	17	18	19	20	21	22	23	24	25	26	27	28

February
Week 6

Saturday 13

Sunday 14
Quadragesima Sunday
St Valentine's Day

Scotch Pancakes with Rhubarb Compote

Rhubarb 400g (14oz), washed and sliced
Stem ginger in syrup 1 piece, drained and finely chopped
Caster sugar 75g (3oz) plus 1 tbsp
Self-raising flour 125g (4½oz)
Egg 1, beaten
Milk 150ml (¼ pint)
Sunflower oil 1 tbsp
Double cream whipped, to serve, optional

1 Tip rhubarb into a saucepan with ginger and 75g (3oz) sugar. Add 1 tbsp water and stir well, slowly bringing to a simmer. Cook gently for 8-10 minutes, stirring often, until fruit is soft.
2 Taste and check the sweetness, adding a little more sugar if necessary. Leave to cool.
3 Sift flour into a bowl and stir in remaining sugar. Make a well in the centre and add egg. Starting in centre, whisk in milk, gradually until smooth and has the consistency of thick cream.

Time 40 mins	**Serves** 4	**Fat** 5g of which	V
	Calories 248	1.2g is saturated	F

4 Wipe a non-stick frying pan with a little oil and heat until hot. Turn down the heat to medium low. Cook pancakes in batches: drop tablespoons of mix into pan, well spaced apart, and fry for 1- 2 minutes on each side until surface puffs and bubbles.
5 Serve pancakes with rhubarb compote and cream, if using.

February

15 Monday

⟩ *First Quarter*

16 Tuesday

17 Wednesday

18 Thursday

19 Friday

M	T	W	T	F	S	S	M	T	W	T	F	S	S
22	23	24	25	26	27	28	29	1	2	3	4	5	6

February
Week 7

Saturday 20

Sunday 21

Roast Beef Hash with Eggs

Rapeseed or olive oil 2 tbsp
Onion 1, peeled and finely chopped
Leftover cooked roast potatoes 350g (12oz), cut into chunks
Cooked roast beef or lamb 225g (8oz), finely chopped
Garlic 2 cloves, peeled and finely chopped
Cayenne pepper or mild chilli powder ¼ tsp
Eggs 4
Mayonnaise 2 tbsp
Chopped parsley 1 tbsp

1 Heat oil in a large non-stick frying pan. Cook onion for 3-4 minutes over a medium heat, until golden brown. Add potatoes, press down and continue to cook for 2-3 minutes without stirring to achieve a crispy base.

2 Stir in cooked meat, garlic, cayenne or chilli powder and season, if required. Reduce heat and cook for about 5 minutes until meat is piping hot.

3 Meanwhile, poach eggs in a separate pan for 3-5 minutes, to your taste.

4 Stir mayonnaise into hash, sprinkle with parsley and serve topped with a poached egg.

Time 20 mins	Serves 4	Fat 35g of which
	Calories 516	7.7g is saturated

February

22 Monday

○ *Full Moon*

23 Tuesday

24 Wednesday

25 Thursday

26 Friday

M	T	W	T	F	S	S	M	T	W	T	F	S	S
29	1	2	3	4	5	6	7	8	9	10	11	12	13

February
Week 8

Saturday **27**

Sunday **28**

Turmeric Pickled Cauliflower

**White/Chinese rice wine
vinegar** 300ml (½ pint)
Caster sugar 2 tbsp
Salt 1 tbsp
Turmeric 1 tsp
Mustard seeds 1 tsp
Crushed dried chillies 1 tsp
Cauliflower 1 small, broken into
florets
Clean jars 1 large or 2 small

1 Pour vinegar into a saucepan
with 200ml (7fl oz) water. Add
sugar and salt and bring up
to boil. Stir until sugar has
dissolved.
2 Add turmeric, mustard seeds
and crushed chillies to liquid.
3 Pack cauliflower into clean
jars, pour in liquid and leave to
cool. Cover and refrigerate for up
to 8 weeks.

Time 15 mins
plus cooling

Makes 2-3 jars
Calories 34

Fat 0.4g of which
0.1g is saturated

V

73

February

M	T	W	T	F	S	S	M	T	W	T	F	S	S
22	23	24	25	26	27	28	**29**	1	2	3	4	5	6

29 Monday

1 Tuesday MARCH

(*Last Quarter*
St David's Day

2 Wednesday

3 Thursday

4 Friday

M	T	W	T	F	S	S	M	T	W	T	F	S	S
7	8	9	10	11	12	13	14	15	16	17	18	19	20

March
Week 9

Saturday 5

Sunday 6
Mothering Sunday
Fourth Sunday in Lent

Chocolate Cookie Sandwiches

Dark chocolate 110g (4oz), broken into pieces
Egg whites 2
Icing sugar 110g (4oz) plus 2 tbsp
Water biscuits or Rich Tea biscuits 110g (4oz), crushed
Double cream 90ml (3fl oz)
Vanilla extract ¼ tsp

1 Preheat oven to 180°C(160°fan)/350°F/Gas 4. Line two baking sheets with non-stick baking paper.

2 Melt chocolate in a heatproof bowl set over a pan of barely simmering water, stirring often.

3 Whisk egg whites until stiff and then continue whisking while gradually adding 110g (4oz) icing sugar.

4 Fold in biscuit crumbs and melted chocolate.

5 Place 20 heaped teaspoonfuls onto baking sheets and flatten slightly. Bake for 10-12 minutes until firm and cracked. Cool a little, then move to a wire rack.

Time 40 mins   **Makes** 10   **Fat** 9g of which 5g is saturated   [V]
Calories 203

6 Whisk cream until softly whipped, then fold in vanilla extract and 1 tbsp icing sugar.

7 Use cream to sandwich cookies together. Dust with icing sugar. Chill until ready to serve.

March

M	T	W	T	F	S	S	M	T	W	T	F	S	S
29	1	2	3	4	5	6	7	8	9	10	11	12	13

7 Monday

8 Tuesday

9 Wednesday

● *New Moon*

10 Thursday

11 Friday

M	T	W	T	F	S	S	M	T	W	T	F	S	S
14	15	16	17	18	19	20	21	22	23	24	25	26	27

March
Week 10

Saturday **12**

Sunday **13**

Cheese & Salmon Filo Parcels

Light soft cheese 110g (4oz)
Wensleydale cheese 110g (4oz), grated
Skinless and boneless red salmon 170g can, drained
Chopped parsley 1 tbsp
Filo pastry 6 sheets
Butter 50g (2oz), melted
Roast vegetables to serve, optional

1 Preheat oven to 200°C(180°fan)/400°F/Gas 6. Grease a baking sheet.
2 Mix together cheeses, salmon and parsley and season.
3 Brush a filo sheet with melted butter and fold in half lengthways. Position so short sides are at top and bottom, then brush with butter and place a spoonful of filling at bottom left corner. Lift right corner over to form a triangle, then fold triangle up and over next part of filo. Continue folding triangle right then left until pastry sheet is completely used up.

Time 30 mins	**Makes** 6	**Fat** 31g of which
	Calories 399	13.7g is saturated

4 Repeat with remaining sheets and filling. Place on baking sheet and brush with butter.

5 Bake for 10 minutes, then serve with roast vegetables, if using.

March

M	T	W	T	F	S	S	M	T	W	T	F	S	S
7	8	9	10	11	12	13	14	15	16	17	18	19	20

14 Monday

15 Tuesday

❯ *First Quarter*

16 Wednesday

17 Thursday

St Patrick's Day
Bank Holiday, N Ireland

18 Friday

M	T	W	T	F	S	S	M	T	W	T	F	S	S
21	22	23	24	25	26	27	28	29	30	31	1	2	3

March
Week 11

Saturday 19

Sunday 20

Vernal equinox
Spring begins
Palm Sunday

Irish Cream Chocolate Trifles

Chocolate Swiss roll 250g (9oz), cut into 6 slices
Bananas 3, peeled and sliced
Fresh custard 500g pot
Double cream 300ml (½ pint)
Irish Cream liqueur 4-5 tbsp
Fudge chunks 50g (2oz)
Dark chocolate sauce to taste

1 Crumble each slice of Swiss roll into six dessert glasses. Arrange banana on top, then cover with custard.
2 Tip cream and liqueur into a bowl and whisk until thickened. Spoon onto custard and sprinkle with fudge chunks. Drizzle with a little chocolate sauce and serve immediately.

Time 15 mins **Serves** 6 **Fat** 35g of which V
Calories 575 19.3g is saturated

March

M	T	W	T	F	S	S	M	T	W	T	F	S	S
14	15	16	17	18	19	20	21	22	23	24	25	26	27

21 Monday

22 Tuesday

23 Wednesday
○ *Full Moon*

24 Thursday

25 Friday
Good Friday
Bank Holiday, UK

M	T	W	T	F	S	S	M	T	W	T	F	S	S
28	29	30	31	1	2	3	4	5	6	7	8	9	10

March
Week 12

Saturday 26
Don't forget to put your clocks forward 1 hour tonight

Sunday 27
British Summer Time begins
Easter Day

Easter Egg Cake Pops

Plain Madeira cake 285g pack
Chocolate spread 5 tbsp
White chocolate 225g (8oz),
broken into pieces
Lollipop sticks 10 x 15cm (6in)
Neon sugar sprinkles

1 Trim off brown edges and crumble cake into a bowl. Add half the chocolate spread and mix well with your hands. Add remaining spread a tablespoon at a time until you have a mixture that can be squished and rolled into 10 tightly packed 30g (1oz) egg shapes.
2 Place on a tray lined with non-stick baking paper and chill for 1 hour.
3 Melt chocolate in a heatproof bowl set over a pan of barely simmering water, stirring often.
4 Dip end of each stick into chocolate and insert into eggs. Place in a cake pop stand or glass and leave to set. Dip cake pop into chocolate and slowly rotate until evenly covered. Hold over a plate and sprinkle with decorations. Leave to set as before. Repeat with other pops.
5 If giving as an Easter gift, pop into a cellophane bag and tie with a pretty coloured ribbon.

Time 30 mins	**Makes** 10	**Fat** 15g of which	V
plus chilling	**Calories** 291	6.5g is saturated	

March

M	T	W	T	F	S	S	M	T	W	T	F	S	S
21	22	23	24	25	26	27	**28**	**29**	**30**	**31**	1	2	3

28 Monday

Easter Monday
Bank Holiday, England, Wales and N Ireland

29 Tuesday

30 Wednesday

31 Thursday

☾ *Last Quarter*

1 Friday APRIL

M	T	W	T	F	S	S	M	T	W	T	F	S	S
4	5	6	7	8	9	10	11	12	13	14	15	16	17

April
Week 13

Saturday 2

Sunday 3
Low Sunday

Hot Cross Bun & Butter Pudding

Hot cross buns 6 large, each sliced into 3 horizontally
Butter 50g (2oz), softened
Apricot jam 175g (6oz)
Double cream 300ml (½ pint)
Milk 300ml (½ pint)
Golden caster sugar 2-3 tbsp
Eggs 4, lightly beaten

1 Spread each slice of bun with butter and jam. Sandwich buns together and cut in half along the diagonal.
2 Butter a 1.7 litre (3 pint) ovenproof dish. Arrange bun triangles neatly in the dish.
3 Pour cream, milk and sugar (if buns are very sweet, use 2 tbsp) into a large saucepan and bring slowly to scalding point, stirring often; do not allow to boil.
4 Pour hot cream onto eggs in a slow and steady stream, whisking constantly. Strain and pour over buns. Leave to soak for an hour.
5 Preheat oven to 190°C(170°fan)/375°F/Gas 5.

Time 1 hr plus soaking	Serves 6 Calories 615	Fat 42g of which 23.5g is saturated	V F

Place pudding into a larger ovenproof dish containing enough water to come halfway up sides of dish and bake for 35-40 minutes or until just set and golden. Serve warm.

83

April

M	T	W	T	F	S	S	M	T	W	T	F	S	S
28	29	30	31	1	2	3	4	5	6	7	8	9	10

4 Monday

5 Tuesday

6 Wednesday

7 Thursday

● *New Moon*

8 Friday

M	T	W	T	F	S	S	M	T	W	T	F	S	S
11	12	13	14	15	16	17	18	19	20	21	22	23	24

April
Week 14

Saturday **9**

Sunday **10**

Notes

April

M	T	W	T	F	S	S	M	T	W	T	F	S	S
4	5	6	7	8	9	10	11	12	13	14	15	16	17

11 Monday

12 Tuesday

13 Wednesday

14 Thursday

) *First Quarter*

15 Friday

M	T	W	T	F	S	S	M	T	W	T	F	S	S
18	19	20	21	22	23	24	25	26	27	28	29	30	1

April
Week 15

Saturday **16**

Sunday **17**

Smoked Haddock & Potato Soup

Smoked haddock fillet 500g (1lb 2oz)
Onion 1, peeled and thinly sliced
Milk 600ml (1 pint)
Potatoes 680g (1½lb), peeled and thickly sliced
Leeks 2, trimmed, washed and sliced
Butter 40g (1½oz), cut into small pieces
Parsley to garnish, optional

1 Place fish in a large saucepan with onion, milk and 600ml (1 pint) water. Bring up to boil then reduce heat, cover and simmer gently for 10 minutes.
2 Meanwhile, cook potatoes in another pan of water for around 15 minutes, until tender. Drain and mash.
3 Strain liquid from fish (reserve fish and onion) and pour into a clean pan. Gradually whisk in mashed potato. Add leeks, bring up to boil then reduce heat, cover and simmer gently for 10 minutes.

Time 40 mins	Serves 4	Fat 12g of which
	Calories 407	7g is saturated

4 Stir butter into soup and season to taste. Flake fish (remove any bones) and add to soup with onion. Reheat gently. Serve garnished with black pepper and parsley, if using.

April

18 Monday

19 Tuesday

20 Wednesday

21 Thursday

Birthday of Queen Elizabeth II

22 Friday

○ *Full Moon*

Saturday 23

St George's Day

Sunday 24

Sticky Lamb Ribs

Onion 1 small, peeled and grated
Ginger ale or cola 300ml (½ pint)
Light soy sauce 2 tbsp
Rapeseed or olive oil 2 tbsp
Garlic 2 cloves, peeled and finely chopped
Runny honey 2 tbsp
Lean lamb ribs 1.3kg (3lb)
Pasta salad to serve, optional

1 In a large non-metallic dish mix all ingredients except ribs together.
2 Toss ribs in marinade and marinate for a minimum of 2 hours, or overnight.
3 Preheat oven to 200°C(180°fan)/400°F/Gas 6. Remove ribs from marinade and transfer to a large non-stick roasting tin. Roast for 1 hour covered with foil, turning once. Remove foil then return to oven, uncovered, for 30 minutes.
4 Serve hot with pasta salad, if using.

Time 1¾ hrs plus marinating

Serves 4
Calories 711

Fat 53g of which 22.5g is saturated

89

April

M	T	W	T	F	S	S	M	T	W	T	F	S	S
18	19	20	21	22	23	24	**25**	**26**	**27**	**28**	**29**	**30**	**1**

25 Monday

26 Tuesday

27 Wednesday

28 Thursday

29 Friday

M	T	W	T	F	S	S	M	T	W	T	F	S	S
2	3	4	5	6	7	8	9	10	11	12	13	14	15

April
Week 17

Saturday 30
(*Last Quarter*

MAY Sunday 1
Rogation Sunday

Florida Prawn Salad

Endive, chard and radiccio salad mix 200g bag
Cooked tiger prawns 350g (12oz), thawed if frozen
Pink grapefruit 2, peeled and segmented, juice reserved
Grapefruit marmalade 3 tbsp
Olive oil 2 tsp
White wine vinegar 2 tsp

1 Divide salad leaves between 4 bowls and top with prawns and grapefruit.
2 Whisk together grapefruit juice, marmalade, olive oil and vinegar. Season to taste, then spoon over salad. Serve immediately.

Time 15 mins   **Serves** 4   **Fat** 2.5g of which
                    Calories 164   0.4g is saturated

91

May

	M	T	W	T	F	S	S	M	T	W	T	F	S	S
	25	26	27	28	29	30	1	2	3	4	5	6	7	8

2 Monday

Bank Holiday, UK

3 Tuesday

4 Wednesday

5 Thursday

Ascension Day
Holy Thursday

6 Friday

● *New Moon*

M	T	W	T	F	S	S	M	T	W	T	F	S	S
9	10	11	12	13	14	15	16	17	18	19	20	21	22

May
Week 18

Saturday **7**

Sunday **8**

Chicken & Avocado Fajitas

Sunflower oil 1 tbsp
Paprika 1 tsp
Cumin ½ tsp
Ground coriander ½ tsp
Chilli powder ½ tsp
Lime 1, zest and juice
Mini chicken breast fillets
350g pack, cut into chunks
Tortilla wraps 6
Cos lettuce ½, shredded
Avocado 1 large, peeled, stoned
and sliced
Chopped coriander 3 tbsp,
optional
Soured cream 4-6 tbsp, optional

1 In a bowl mix together oil,
spices, lime zest and juice and
use to coat chicken. Heat a non-
stick frying pan and fry chicken
over a medium-high heat for
about 5 minutes, until cooked.
2 Warm wraps according to
packet's instructions. Divide
lettuce and avocado between
them, top with chicken,
coriander and soured cream, if
using, roll up and serve.

Time 20 mins   **Serves** 3   **Fat** 19g of which
    Calories 598   5.7g is saturated

93

May

M	T	W	T	F	S	S	M	T	W	T	F	S	S
2	3	4	5	6	7	8	9	10	11	12	13	14	15

9 Monday

10 Tuesday

11 Wednesday

12 Thursday

13 Friday

) *First Quarter*

M	T	W	T	F	S	S	M	T	W	T	F	S	S
16	17	18	19	20	21	22	23	24	25	26	27	28	29

May
Week 19

Saturday 14

Sunday 15
Whit Sunday
Pentecost

Cod in a Light Curry Sauce

Cod or haddock fillet 2 x 225g (8oz) fillets
Onion 1, peeled and finely chopped
Sunflower oil 1 tbsp
Curry paste 1 tbsp
Beefsteak tomatoes 2, skinned and chopped
Apricot jam 2 tbsp
Single cream 4 tbsp
Cooked rice, naan bread and coriander to serve, optional

1 Preheat oven to 220°C(200°fan)/425°F/Gas 7. Place fish fillets onto a sheet of oiled foil on a baking sheet. Season and then enclose fish in the foil and bake for 15-20 minutes until just cooked.
2 Meanwhile, cook onion gently in oil for 5 minutes until softened. Add curry paste and tomatoes, cover and cook gently for 10-15 minutes until tomatoes are soft and pulpy.
3 Stir in jam and cream and heat through gently.

Time 30 mins	**Serves** 2	**Fat** 15g of which
	Calories 428	4.7g is saturated

4 Break cooked fish fillets into chunks and stir into curry sauce. Season to taste, then serve immediately with cooked rice and warm naan bread. Garnish with coriander, if using.

95

16 Monday

17 Tuesday

18 Wednesday

19 Thursday

20 Friday

Saturday 21

○ *Full Moon*

Sunday 22

Trinity Sunday

Spicy Sausage & Tomato Pasta

Olive oil 1 tbsp
Pork sausages 4-6, cut into chunks
Onion 1 small, peeled and finely chopped
Garlic 1 clove, peeled and finely chopped
Dried chilli flakes ¼-½ tsp
Chopped tomatoes 400g can
Red kidney beans 215g can, rinsed and drained
Dried fusilli 150g (5oz)
Grated Parmesan and basil leaves to serve, optional

1 Heat oil in a non-stick frying pan and cook sausage for 10 minutes until golden brown, stirring. Add onion and cook for 5 minutes, stirring frequently. Add garlic and dried chilli flakes and cook for a further minute.
2 Pour in tomatoes and beans. Bring up to boil, reduce the heat and simmer gently for 10 minutes or until mixture has thickened and sausages are cooked, stirring often.

Time 35 mins	**Serves** 2	**Fat** 35g of which	F
	Calories 832	11g is saturated	

3 Meanwhile, cook fusilli in a large saucepan of lightly salted boiling water according to packet's instructions. When pasta is al dente, drain well.

4 Tip pasta into frying pan with sausage. Stir well to coat and season. Spoon onto plates and sprinkle with Parmesan and basil leaves, if using.

May

	M	T	W	T	F	S	S	M	T	W	T	F	S	S
	16	17	18	19	20	21	22	23	24	25	26	27	28	29

23 Monday

24 Tuesday

25 Wednesday

26 Thursday

Corpus Christi

27 Friday

M	T	W	T	F	S	S	M	T	W	T	F	S	S
30	31	1	2	3	4	5	6	7	8	9	10	11	12

May
Week 21

Saturday 28

Sunday 29
(*Last Quarter*

Strawberry Jellies

Strawberries 625g (1lb 6oz), hulled and sliced
Caster sugar 50g (2oz)
Powdered gelatine 3 tsp
Lemon 1, juice only
Sugar flowers to decorate, optional

1 Place 400g (14oz) of strawberries into a saucepan with sugar and 125ml (4fl oz) water. Cover and cook gently for around 5 minutes until fruit has softened.
2 Meanwhile, pour 4 tbsp water into a small heatproof bowl and sprinkle with gelatine. Leave to soak for 5 minutes.
3 Purée cooked strawberries with their juice in a blender and then pass through a sieve to remove seeds.
4 Heat gelatine over a pan of barely simmering water until it forms a clear liquid. Stir this liquid into strawberry fruit purée with lemon juice then leave purée to cool.

Time 30 mins plus chilling	Serves 6 Calories 70	Fat 0.1g of which 0g is saturated

5 Stir in remaining fruit then pour into six 150ml (¼ pint) cups. Chill for 4 hours until set.

6 Dip in hot water for 10 seconds then turn out onto plates. Add sugar flowers.

May

M	T	W	T	F	S	S	M	T	W	T	F	S	S
23	24	25	26	27	28	29	30	31	1	2	3	4	5

30 Monday

Bank Holiday, UK

31 Tuesday

1 Wednesday JUNE

2 Thursday

Coronation Day

3 Friday

M	T	W	T	F	S	S	M	T	W	T	F	S	S
6	7	8	9	10	11	12	13	14	15	16	17	18	19

June
Week 22

Saturday 4

Sunday 5

● *New Moon*

Maids of Honour

Shortcrust pastry 500g packet
Quark 250g tub
Eggs 2 large
Soft light brown sugar
110g (4oz)
Single cream 4 tbsp
Brandy 2 tbsp
Ground almonds 150g (5oz)
Raisins 50g (2oz), chopped
Icing sugar for sifting

1 Preheat oven to
220°C(200°fan)/425°F/Gas 7.
On a lightly floured surface,
roll out pastry to a thickness
just less than a one pence piece.
Using a 8.5cm (3¼in) fluted
cutter, stamp out 24 rounds
from pastry, re-rolling trimmings
when necessary.
2 Line two deep-hole bun tins
with pastry rounds and chill
while making filling.
3 Beat together quark, eggs,
brown sugar, cream, brandy and
ground almonds. Stir in chopped
raisins and then spoon into
pastry cases.

Time 40 mins	**Makes** 24	**Fat** 10g of which	V
	Calories 180	2.6g is saturated	

4 Bake for 15-20 minutes until
well risen, golden brown and
firm to touch. Allow to cool

slightly then transfer to a wire
rack to cool completely. Sift with
icing sugar and serve.

June

M	T	W	T	F	S	S	M	T	W	T	F	S	S
30	31	1	2	3	4	5	6	7	8	9	10	11	12

6 Monday

7 Tuesday

8 Wednesday

9 Thursday

10 Friday

Birthday of Prince Philip, Duke of Edinburgh

M	T	W	T	F	S	S	M	T	W	T	F	S	S
13	14	15	16	17	18	19	20	21	22	23	24	25	26

June
Week 23

Saturday **11**

Sunday **12**
〉 *First Quarter*

Minted Pea Panna Cotta with Smoked Salmon

Frozen petits pois or fresh peas 250g (9oz) plus extra to garnish
Chicken stock 250ml (9fl oz)
Leaf gelatine 2 sheets
Double cream 150ml (¼ pint)
Mint leaves 12-15 plus extra to garnish
Smoked salmon 100g pack

1 Place petits pois and stock in a saucepan. Bring up to boil, cover and simmer for 5 minutes.
2 Meanwhile, soak gelatine sheets in a bowl of cold water.
3 Stir cream into peas, add mint leaves, then liquidise and pass through a sieve. Season to taste.
4 Drain gelatine sheets and add to pea cream. Briefly heat gently until gelatine dissolves.
5 Lightly oil two ramekin dishes and pour in pea cream. Allow to cool then chill for 4-6 hours.
6 Run a knife around the inside of each ramekin and turn out onto plates. Serve with salmon garnished with mint and peas.

Time 20 mins plus chilling	**Serves** 2 **Calories** 539	**Fat** 44g of which 25.6g is saturated

103

June

M	T	W	T	F	S	S	M	T	W	T	F	S	S
6	7	8	9	10	11	12	13	14	15	16	17	18	19

13 Monday

14 Tuesday

15 Wednesday

16 Thursday

17 Friday

M	T	W	T	F	S	S	M	T	W	T	F	S	S
20	21	22	23	24	25	26	27	28	29	30	1	2	3

June
Week 24

Saturday **18**

Sunday **19**

Father's Day

Lamb Keema Curry

Onion 1, peeled and chopped
Garlic 2 cloves, peeled and chopped
Root ginger 2.5cm (1in), peeled and grated
Minced lamb 500g (1lb 2oz)
Chopped tomatoes 400g can
Cumin 2 tsp
Turmeric 1 tsp
Garam masala 1 tbsp
Chilli powder ½-1 tsp
Raisins 50g (2oz)
Frozen peas 50g (2oz)
Cooked rice, fat-free Greek yogurt and fresh mint to serve, optional

1 Gently fry onion, garlic and ginger with lamb until softened and meat is browned all over.
2 Pour in chopped tomatoes with 100ml (3½fl oz) water and all spices. Cover and simmer for 30 minutes.
3 Add raisins and peas and cook for a further 15 minutes.
4 Serve on a bed of rice topped with yogurt and shredded mint.

Time 1 hr   **Serves** 4   **Fat** 18g of which   F
 Calories 335   7.8g is saturated

105

June

M	T	W	T	F	S	S	M	T	W	T	F	S	S
13	14	15	16	17	18	19	**20**	**21**	**22**	**23**	**24**	**25**	**26**

20 Monday

○ *Full Moon*
Summer solstice
Summer begins

21 Tuesday

22 Wednesday

23 Thursday

24 Friday

M	T	W	T	F	S	S	M	T	W	T	F	S	S
27	28	29	30	1	2	3	4	5	6	7	8	9	10

June
Week 25

Saturday 25

Sunday 26

Homebaked Sally Lunns

Strong plain flour 500g (1lb 2oz)
Fast-acting dried yeast 7g sachet
Salt 1 tsp
Eggs 2, beaten
Butter 50g (2oz), melted
Milk 300ml (½ pint), warmed to blood temperature
Ham or cheese and salad to serve

1 Tip flour into a bowl and stir in yeast and salt. Reserve 1 tbsp of beaten egg and beat the rest into flour with butter and enough milk to make a soft dough. Knead for 10 minutes on a floured surface.

2 Preheat oven to 220°C(200°fan)/425°F/Gas 7. Lightly butter two 18cm (7in) sandwich tins.

3 Divide dough in half and shape each into a flattish round ball. Place in tins, cover with oiled clingfilm and leave in a warm place until doubled in size.

4 Brush top of loaves with reserved egg and bake for 15-20 minutes until risen and golden. Loaves should sound hollow when tapped on base.

5 Transfer to a wire rack to cool. Serve warm or cold, cut in two and filled with ham or cheese and salad.

Time 35 mins plus proving	**Serves** 4 **Calories** 598	**Fat** 15g of which 7.8g is saturated	

June

	M	T	W	T	F	S	S	M	T	W	T	F	S	S
	20	21	22	23	24	25	26	27	28	29	30	1	2	3

27 Monday
(*Last Quarter*

28 Tuesday

29 Wednesday

30 Thursday

1 Friday JULY

M	T	W	T	F	S	S	M	T	W	T	F	S	S
4	5	6	7	8	9	10	11	12	13	14	15	16	17

July
Week 26

Saturday **2**

Sunday **3**

Blueberry Bircher Muesli

Greek yogurt 500g tub
Rolled oats 200g (7oz)
**Wheatgerm or ground
hazelnuts** 40g (1½oz)
Desiccated coconut 40g (1½oz)
Hazelnuts 50g (2oz), toasted
and chopped
Cloudy apple juice 200ml
(7fl oz)
To serve per portion
Granny Smith apple ½, cored
but not peeled, coarsely grated
Blueberries 50g (2oz)
Runny honey 1 tsp
Ground cinnamon to sprinkle

1 Mix together yogurt, oats and
wheatgerm or ground hazelnuts
then stir in coconut, hazelnuts
and juice. Transfer to a container,
clip on lid and chill overnight.
2 When ready to serve, stir in
apple and a few blueberries and
spoon into glasses. Top with
blueberries, honey and cinnamon.
3 The remaining muesli will keep
in the fridge for 2-3 days; just
add a little juice, if required.

Time 10 mins	**Serves** 6	**Fat** 22g of which
plus chilling	**Calories** 422	9.7g is saturated

July

	M	T	W	T	F	S	S	M	T	W	T	F	S	S
	27	28	29	30	1	2	3	4	5	6	7	8	9	10

4 Monday

● *New Moon*

5 Tuesday

6 Wednesday

7 Thursday

8 Friday

Saturday **9**

Sunday **10**

Notes

July

M	T	W	T	F	S	S	M	T	W	T	F	S	S
4	5	6	7	8	9	10	11	12	13	14	15	16	17

11 Monday

12 Tuesday

) *First Quarter*
Bank Holiday, N Ireland

13 Wednesday

14 Thursday

15 Friday

M	T	W	T	F	S	S	M	T	W	T	F	S	S
18	19	20	21	22	23	24	25	26	27	28	29	30	31

July
Week 28

Saturday 16

Sunday 17

Tuna, Avocado & Fennel Salad

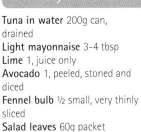

Tuna in water 200g can, drained
Light mayonnaise 3-4 tbsp
Lime 1, juice only
Avocado 1, peeled, stoned and diced
Fennel bulb ½ small, very thinly sliced
Salad leaves 60g packet

1 Mix together tuna, mayonnaise and lime juice.
2 Add avocado, season to taste and gently stir together.
3 Divide salad leaves between two plates. Spoon tuna mix on top.

Time 10 mins	**Serves** 2	**Fat** 20g of which
	Calories 296	3.7g is saturated

July

M	T	W	T	F	S	S	M	T	W	T	F	S	S
11	12	13	14	15	16	17	**18**	**19**	**20**	**21**	**22**	**23**	**24**

18 Monday

19 Tuesday

○ *Full Moon*

20 Wednesday

21 Thursday

22 Friday

M	T	W	T	F	S	S	M	T	W	T	F	S	S
25	26	27	28	29	30	31	1	2	3	4	5	6	7

July
Week 29

Saturday **23**

Sunday **24**

Parmigiano Reggiano Herby Potato Wedges

Potatoes 3 large, scrubbed and cut into wedges
Olive oil 2 tbsp
Chopped rosemary 2½ tbsp
Parmigiano Reggiano 75g (3oz), grated

1 Preheat oven to 200°C(180°fan)/400°F/Gas 6.
2 Toss potatoes in oil, rosemary, most of the Parmigiano Reggiano and black pepper.
3 Place on a non-stick baking sheet and bake for 40-50 minutes or until cooked through and golden brown.
4 Serve sprinkled with a little more Parmigiano Reggiano.

Time 1 hr

Serves 4
Calories 225

Fat 12g of which 4.4g is saturated

July

M	T	W	T	F	S	S	M	T	W	T	F	S	S
18	19	20	21	22	23	24	25	26	27	28	29	30	31

25 Monday

26 Tuesday
☾ *Last Quarter*

27 Wednesday

28 Thursday

29 Friday

Saturday 30

Sunday 31

Lamb, Apricot & Coriander Burgers

Minced lamb 450g (1lb)
Dried apricots 25g (1oz), finely chopped
Shelled pistachio nuts 25g (1oz), finely chopped, optional
Chopped coriander or mint 1 tbsp
Lemon ½, grated zest and juice
Ciabatta buns, salad and relish to serve

1 In a large bowl, mix first five ingredients together. Season.
2 Using slightly damp hands shape mixture into four 9cm (3½in) burgers. Cover and chill for 20 minutes.
3 Cook burgers on a barbecue or under a moderate grill for 6-8 minutes on each side until cooked and any juices run clear.
4 Serve in a ciabatta bun with salad and relish.

Time 30 mins plus chilling
Makes 4
Calories 326
Fat 19g of which 7.6g is saturated
F

August

M	T	W	T	F	S	S	M	T	W	T	F	S	S
25	26	27	28	29	30	31	1	2	3	4	5	6	7

1 Monday AUGUST

Bank Holiday, Scotland

2 Tuesday

● *New Moon*

3 Wednesday

4 Thursday

5 Friday

M	T	W	T	F	S	S	M	T	W	T	F	S	S
8	9	10	11	12	13	14	15	16	17	18	19	20	21

August
Week 31

Saturday **6**

Sunday **7**

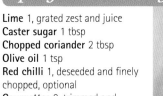

Spicy Lime Courgettes

Lime 1, grated zest and juice
Caster sugar 1 tbsp
Chopped coriander 2 tbsp
Olive oil 1 tsp
Red chilli 1, deseeded and finely chopped, optional
Courgettes 2, trimmed and grated

1 Mix together lime zest and juice, sugar, coriander, olive oil, 1 tbsp boiling water and chilli, if using.
2 Toss dressing though grated courgettes and leave for 10 minutes for flavours to develop. Serve with cold meat or as a barbecue accompaniment.

Time 15 mins **Serves** 4 **Fat** 1.3g of which [V]
Calories 43 0.2g is saturated

119

August

M	T	W	T	F	S	S	M	T	W	T	F	S	S
1	2	3	4	5	6	7	8	9	10	11	12	13	14

8 Monday

9 Tuesday

10 Wednesday

❭ *First Quarter*

11 Thursday

12 Friday

M	T	W	T	F	S	S	M	T	W	T	F	S	S
15	16	17	18	19	20	21	22	23	24	25	26	27	28

August
Week 32

Saturday 13

Sunday 14

Cumberland Scotch Eggs

Eggs 6
White bread 2 slices, crusts removed
Milk 4 tbsp
Cumberland sausages 500g (1lb 2oz)
Chopped parsley 2 tbsp
Grated nutmeg
Streaky bacon 6 rashers, stretched

1 Boil water in a saucepan and then add eggs. Bring back to boil and simmer for 5 minutes. Cool under cold running water.
2 Preheat oven to 190°C(170°fan)/375°F/Gas 5. Shell eggs and set aside.
3 Place bread in a large bowl and pour in milk. Leave to soak for 2 minutes, then mash with your hands.
4 Remove meat from sausage skins and add to bread with parsley, a grating of nutmeg and seasoning. Work together with wet hands and divide into 6 balls then flatten to make rounds.

Time 1¼ hrs	Makes 6	Fat 33g of which
	Calories 425	11.5g is saturated

5 Stand an egg in centre of each round and lift together to form a ball and seal egg. Place in a muffin tin and criss-cross 2 pieces of bacon over top.

6 Bake for 35 minutes, then leave for 5 minutes in tin. Remove from tin and serve warm or cold with salad for lunch or as part of a picnic.

August

M	T	W	T	F	S	S	M	T	W	T	F	S	S
8	9	10	11	12	13	14	15	16	17	18	19	20	21

15 Monday

16 Tuesday

17 Wednesday

18 Thursday

○ *Full Moon*

19 Friday

M	T	W	T	F	S	S	M	T	W	T	F	S	S
22	23	24	25	26	27	28	29	30	31	1	2	3	4

August
Week 33

Saturday **20**

Sunday **21**

Cornish Fairings

Plain flour 110g (4oz)
Salt ¼ tsp
Baking powder 1 tsp
Bicarbonate of soda 1 tsp
Ground ginger 1 tsp
Mixed spice 1 tsp
Butter 50g (2oz)
Granulated sugar 50g (2oz)
Lemon 1, finely grated zest
Golden syrup 2 tbsp

1 Preheat oven to 200°C(180°fan)/400°F/Gas 6. Grease two baking sheets.
2 Sift flour, salt, baking powder, bicarbonate of soda and spices into a bowl. Rub in butter, then stir in sugar and zest. Mix in syrup to a soft, not sticky dough.
3 Roll half the mixture into walnut-sized balls and place on baking sheet, leaving room to spread. Bake on top shelf of oven but after 5-6 minutes, when they begin to colour, move to lower shelf for 1-2 minutes where they will crack. Cool on a wire rack. Repeat with remaining mixture.

| **Time** 30 mins | **Makes** 15 | **Fat** 3g of which | V |
| | **Calories** 74 | 1.8g is saturated | F |

123

August

22 Monday

23 Tuesday

24 Wednesday

25 Thursday

(*Last Quarter*

26 Friday

M	T	W	T	F	S	S	M	T	W	T	F	S	S
29	30	31	1	2	3	4	5	6	7	8	9	10	11

August
Week 34

Saturday **27**

Sunday **28**

Salmon with Roast Red Pepper Salad

Olive oil 2-3 tbsp
Lemon 1, juice only
Salmon fillets 2, about 150g (5oz) each
Red pepper 1, halved, deseeded and finely sliced
Red onion 1 small, peeled and thinly sliced
Garlic 1 clove, peeled and finely chopped
Chopped parsley 1 tbsp
Lime and coriander basmati rice 250g packet

1 Preheat oven to 220°C(200°fan)/425°F/Gas 7 and line a roasting tin with foil.
2 Mix together 1 tbsp of oil and lemon juice, then season well.
3 Place salmon in centre of foil and drizzle with oil mix. Wrap tightly and bake for 15 minutes or until salmon is cooked.
4 Meanwhile, in a separate roasting tin, toss pepper in remaining oil, season, and roast for 15 minutes until pepper is just tender, turning occasionally.

Time 30 mins	Serves 2	Fat 28g of which
	Calories 399	4.5g is saturated

5 Remove pepper from oven and tip into a bowl with onion, garlic and parsley and season to taste.

6 Cook rice according to packet's instructions and serve with salmon and salad.

August

M	T	W	T	F	S	S	M	T	W	T	F	S	S
22	23	24	25	26	27	28	**29**	**30**	**31**	1	2	3	4

29 Monday

Bank Holiday, England, Wales and N Ireland

30 Tuesday

31 Wednesday

1 Thursday SEPTEMBER

● *New Moon*

2 Friday

M	T	W	T	F	S	S	M	T	W	T	F	S	S
5	6	7	8	9	10	11	12	13	14	15	16	17	18

September
Week 35

Saturday 3

Sunday 4

Coconut Raspberry Friands

Butter 75g (3oz)
Lemon ½, grated zest only
Egg whites 3
Icing sugar 110g (4oz) plus extra to sift
Plain flour 40g (1½oz), sifted
Desiccated coconut 50g (2oz)
Ground almonds 25g (1oz)
Raspberries 110g (4oz)

1 Preheat oven to 200°C(180°fan)/400°F/Gas 6. Oil and base line six individual 150ml (¼ pint) metal friand or mini loaf tins then put the tins on a baking sheet (alternatively use a 12 hole deep muffin tin).

2 Melt butter with lemon zest in a small saucepan then leave to cool.

3 Whisk egg whites in a large bowl until stiff peaks form then gradually whisk in sugar a little at a time and continue to whisk until smooth and glossy.

4 Add flour, coconut and almonds and gently fold together. Fold in melted butter.

Time 40 mins	**Makes** 6	**Fat** 18g of which
	Calories 275	11g is saturated

5 Divide mixture between tins and smooth surfaces. Press in 4 or 5 raspberries. Bake for 15-20 minutes until tops are golden and a skewer comes out cleanly.

6 Leave to cool for 5 minutes then turn out on to a wire rack and dust with a little icing sugar. Serve warm or cold on their own or with a drizzle of cream.

127

September

5 Monday

6 Tuesday

7 Wednesday

8 Thursday

9 Friday

⟩ *First Quarter*

M	T	W	T	F	S	S	M	T	W	T	F	S	S
12	13	14	15	16	17	18	19	20	21	22	23	24	25

September
Week 36

Saturday **10**

Sunday **11**

Beetroot Risotto

Butter 25g (1oz)
Onion 1 small, peeled and finely chopped
Garlic 1 clove, peeled and finely chopped
Arborio or risotto rice 175g (6oz)
White wine 100ml (3½fl oz)
Ready-to-eat beetroot 250g pack (not in vinegar), drained and chopped in a food processor
Hot vegetable stock 500ml (18fl oz)
Parmesan 25g (1oz)
Blue or goat's cheese 50g (2oz), crumbled, optional

1 Melt butter in a large pan and gently cook chopped onion and garlic for 5 minutes until softened but not browned.
2 Add rice to pan and stir to coat. Pour in wine and stir until absorbed.
3 Add ¼ of beetroot to pan with a ladleful of hot stock. Stir until absorbed. Add remaining stock a ladleful at a time, stirring over a low heat until each ladleful is absorbed. Add remaining beetroot with final ladleful.
4 Stir through Parmesan, season to taste and serve immediately topped with cheese, if using.

Time 45 mins   **Serves** 2   **Fat** 17g of which 8.9g is saturated
Calories 561

129

September

12 Monday

13 Tuesday

14 Wednesday

15 Thursday

16 Friday

○ *Full Moon*

M	T	W	T	F	S	S	M	T	W	T	F	S	S
19	20	21	22	23	24	25	26	27	28	29	30	1	2

September
Week 37

Saturday **17**

Sunday **18**

Pear & Ginger Sorbet

Caster sugar 150g (5oz)
Canned pears in natural juice
2 x 420g cans
Stem ginger in syrup 2 pieces,
drained
Lemon 1, zest only
Amaretti biscuits to serve,
optional

1 Put sugar in a small pan with 150ml (¼ pint) of juice from pears. Bring up to boil and then boil for 5 minutes. Leave to cool slightly.
2 Place pears, stem ginger and lemon zest in a food processor. Add cooled sugar syrup and purée until smooth.
3 Spoon into a freezer-proof container and freeze for 2 hours. Mash with a fork and return to freezer. Repeat until softly frozen (about 6 hours).
4 Serve with Amaretti biscuits, if using.

| **Time** 15 mins plus freezing | **Serves** 6 **Calories** 142 | **Fat** 0.1g of which 0g is saturated | V F |

September

19 Monday

20 Tuesday

21 Wednesday

22 Thursday

Autumnal equinox
Autumn begins

23 Friday

(*Last Quarter*

M	T	W	T	F	S	S	M	T	W	T	F	S	S
26	27	28	29	30	1	2	3	4	5	6	7	8	9

September
Week 38

Saturday **24**

Sunday **25**

Spaghetti Soup with Pesto

Onion 1 small, peeled and sliced
Carrot 1, peeled and diced
Olive oil 1 tbsp
Mushrooms 4-6, wiped and chopped
Chopped tomatoes 227g can
Vegetable stock cube 1
Angel hair spaghetti or rice noodles 25g (1oz)
Pesto 1 tbsp
Grated Parmesan cheese 1 tbsp

1 In a large saucepan cook onion and carrot in oil for about 5 minutes until softened.
2 Add mushrooms and cook for 3 minutes more.
3 Pour in tomatoes, add stock cube and 600ml (1 pint) boiling water and bring up to boil. Cover and simmer for 15 minutes.
4 Break spaghetti or noodles into pieces and add to pan, then boil, uncovered, for 3 minutes or until pasta is cooked.
5 Stir in half of pesto and season. Ladle into bowls and top with pesto and Parmesan cheese.

Time 40 mins **Serves** 3 **Fat** 12g of which F
 Calories 218 2.6g is saturated

September

M	T	W	T	F	S	S	M	T	W	T	F	S	S
19	20	21	22	23	24	25	26	27	28	29	30	1	2

26 Monday

Don't forget to order your 2017 Dairy Diary. Use the order form on page 170 or order online.
If you don't have a milkman, call 0845 0948 128 or visit www.dairydiary.co.uk

27 Tuesday

28 Wednesday

29 Thursday

30 Friday

M	T	W	T	F	S	S	M	T	W	T	F	S	S
3	4	5	6	7	8	9	10	11	12	13	14	15	16

October
Week 39

OCTOBER Saturday **1**

● *New Moon*

Sunday **2**

Notes

October

3 Monday

4 Tuesday

5 Wednesday

6 Thursday

7 Friday

M	T	W	T	F	S	S	M	T	W	T	F	S	S
10	11	12	13	14	15	16	17	18	19	20	21	22	23

October
Week 40

Saturday 8

Sunday 9

⟩ *First Quarter*

Gorgonzola Dolce & Apple Pizzas

Pizza base mix 145g packet
Crème fraîche 3-4 tbsp
Red onion 1 small, finely chopped
Dessert apples 2, thinly sliced
Chopped sage 2 tbsp plus extra leaves to garnish
Gorgonzola Dolce 120g (4½oz)

1 Preheat oven to 240°C(220°fan)/475°F/Gas 9. Make pizza dough according to pack's instructions and then shape into four small flat rounds, the size of a saucer.

2 Spread a thin layer of crème fraîche over each base, leaving a rim around the edge. Sprinkle with onion and top with apple slices and sage. Season to taste before scattering over Gorgonzola Dolce.

3 Bake for 15-20 minutes until golden and base is cooked through. Serve scattered with fresh sage.

Time 40 mins
Makes 4
Calories 286
Fat 16g of which 9.3g is saturated

137

October

M	T	W	T	F	S	S	M	T	W	T	F	S	S
3	4	5	6	7	8	9	10	11	12	13	14	15	16

10 Monday

11 Tuesday

12 Wednesday

13 Thursday

14 Friday

M	T	W	T	F	S	S	M	T	W	T	F	S	S
17	18	19	20	21	22	23	24	25	26	27	28	29	30

October
Week 41

Saturday 15

Sunday 16
○ *Full Moon*

Parmigiano Reggiano Duck Ragu

Duck legs 2, skin on
Olive oil 1 tbsp
Onion 1 small, peeled and finely chopped
Celery 1 stick, finely chopped
Garlic 3 cloves, peeled and crushed
Tomato purée 3 tbsp
Dried Italian herbs ½ tsp
Snipped thyme leaves 1 tbsp plus extra leaves to garnish
Chopped tomatoes 400g can
Dark brown sugar 2 tsp
Red wine 150ml (¼ pint)
Cooked pasta shapes 75g (3oz)
Parmigiano Reggiano 75g (3oz)

1 Preheat oven to 180°C(160°fan)/350°F/Gas 4. Rub duck in oil, season and place on a baking tray. Roast for 40-50 minutes until meat is tender.
2 Leave to cool and reserve fat. Shred meat and discard bones.
3 Heat duck fat in a heavy-based saucepan and gently cook onion, celery and garlic for around 5 minutes until softened.

| **Time** 2 hrs | **Serves** 2 | **Fat** 65g of which |
| | **Calories** 951 | 21.4g is saturated |

4 Stir in tomato purée, herbs, tomatoes, sugar and wine. Bring up to boil, stir in meat and then simmer for 45 minutes or until sauce has reduced. Season.

5 Stir pasta through ragu along with 40g (1½oz) Parmigiano Reggiano. Serve topped with remaining Parmigiano Reggiano and thyme leaves.

139

October

17 Monday

18 Tuesday

19 Wednesday

20 Thursday

21 Friday

M	T	W	T	F	S	S	M	T	W	T	F	S	S
24	25	26	27	28	29	30	31	1	2	3	4	5	6

October
Week 42

Saturday **22**

(*Last Quarter*

Sunday **23**

Win Four Fabulous Fragrant Yankee Candles

If only this were a scratch and sniff page! These candles smell absolutely divine and could be scenting your home with their delicious fragrances if you enter our prize draw. We have four large jar candles to give away; one Honey Glow, one Wild Fig, one Ginger Dusk and one Amber Moon.

To enter visit
www.dairydiary.co.uk/win2016
If you don't use the internet you can enter by sending your name and address to:
Yankee Candle Competition Eaglemoss Consumer Publications, Electra House, Electra Way, Crewe, CW1 6GL.
Closing date:
30th November 2016.

You can order your 2017 Dairy Diary via your milkman (see p170), online at www.dairydiary.co.uk or by calling 0845 0948 128.

October

24 Monday

25 Tuesday

26 Wednesday

27 Thursday

28 Friday

M	T	W	T	F	S	S	M	T	W	T	F	S	S
31	1	2	3	4	5	6	7	8	9	10	11	12	13

October
Week 43

Saturday 29

Don't forget to put your clocks back 1 hour tonight

Sunday 30

● *New Moon*
British Summer Time ends

Trick or Treat Toffee Apples

Apples 6 small
Granulated sugar 250g (9oz)
Golden syrup 2 tbsp
White wine vinegar 1 tbsp
Butter 25g (1oz)
Wooden lollipop sticks 6

1 Press a wooden stick into the stalk end of each apple.
2 Pour 125ml (4fl oz) water into a saucepan and add sugar, golden syrup and vinegar. Stir over a low heat until sugar dissolves. Increase heat and boil rapidly for 10 minutes until a little of the mixture separates into hard brittle threads when dropped into a cup of cold water.
3 Remove from heat and stir in butter. Stand pan in cold water to prevent it cooking further.
4 Dip each apple into syrup and stand on a piece of baking paper. Reheat toffee gently if it becomes too sticky. Dip apples again, if desired.
5 Eat immediately or wrap in cellophane.

| **Time** 20 mins | **Makes** 6 | **Fat** 3g of which | V |
| | **Calories** 195 | 2g is saturated | |

143

October

M	T	W	T	F	S	S	M	T	W	T	F	S	S
24	25	26	27	28	29	30	31	1	2	3	4	5	6

31 Monday

Halloween

1 Tuesday NOVEMBER

2 Wednesday

3 Thursday

4 Friday

M	T	W	T	F	S	S	M	T	W	T	F	S	S
7	8	9	10	11	12	13	14	15	16	17	18	19	20

November
Week 44

Saturday 5
Bonfire Night

Sunday 6

Peanut Butter Hot Chocolate

Milk chocolate 40g (1½oz), broken up
Smooth peanut butter 2 tbsp
Milk 350ml (12fl oz)
Whipped cream 2 tbsp, optional
Mini marshmallows and grated chocolate to serve, optional

1 Place chocolate, peanut butter and milk in a pan. Heat gently, whisking, until chocolate has melted and mixture is smooth.
2 Pour into 2 mugs and top with whipped cream and marshmallows and/or grated chocolate, if using.

Time 10 mins	**Serves** 2	**Fat** 17g of which	V
	Calories 282	7.6g is saturated	

145

November

M	T	W	T	F	S	S	M	T	W	T	F	S	S
31	1	2	3	4	5	6	7	8	9	10	11	12	13

7 Monday

❯ *First Quarter*

8 Tuesday

9 Wednesday

10 Thursday

11 Friday

M	T	W	T	F	S	S	M	T	W	T	F	S	S
14	15	16	17	18	19	20	21	22	23	24	25	26	27

November
Week 45

Saturday 12

Sunday 13
Remembrance Sunday

Chorizo & Cheddar Scones

Self-raising flour 225g (8oz)
Butter 50g (2oz)
Cheddar cheese 50g (2oz), grated
Chorizo 40g (1½oz), chopped
Milk 150ml (¼ pint) plus extra to glaze

1 Preheat oven to 230°C(210°fan)/450°F/Gas 8. Line a baking tray with baking paper.
2 Sift flour into a large bowl, then rub in butter until it resembles fine breadcrumbs.
3 Stir cheese and chorizo into flour. Then add milk and mix to a soft but not sticky dough.
4 Turn onto a lightly floured surface and knead until smooth.
5 Roll out to 2cm (¾in) thick and cut out rounds with a 7.5cm (3in) circular cutter. Repeat until dough is used up.
6 Place on baking sheet and brush tops with milk. Bake for 12-15 minutes until well risen and golden. Cool slightly on a wire rack. Serve warm or cold.

Time 30 mins	**Makes** 8	**Fat** 7.3g of which	F
	Calories 151	4.3g is saturated	

147

November

M	T	W	T	F	S	S	M	T	W	T	F	S	S
7	8	9	10	11	12	13	**14**	**15**	**16**	17	18	**19**	20

14 Monday

○ *Full Moon*
Birthday of the Prince of Wales

15 Tuesday

16 Wednesday

17 Thursday

18 Friday

M	T	W	T	F	S	S	M	T	W	T	F	S	S
21	22	23	24	25	26	27	28	29	30	1	2	3	4

November
Week 46

Saturday **19**

Sunday **20**

Caramelised Pear & Stilton Salad

Olive oil 2 tsp
Butter 15g (½oz)
Large ripe Conference pear 1, cored and cut into eighths
Caster sugar 1 tsp
Balsamic vinegar 1 tbsp
Prepared wild rocket and salad leaves 50g (2oz)
Stilton 75g (3oz), crumbled
Walnut pieces 25g (1oz)

1 Heat oil and butter in a non-stick frying pan. Add pear slices and cook for 2-3 minutes on each side until just golden. Sprinkle with sugar and cook for a further 2 minutes until pears begin to caramelise. Remove from the pan and set aside.
2 Turn off the heat and add vinegar to the pan, mixing with juices to form a dressing.
3 Divide salad leaves between two plates, arrange pear slices on top, scatter Stilton and walnuts over and drizzle with a little dressing. Season to taste.

Time 15 mins   **Serves** 2   **Fat** 39g of which 15g is saturated   [V]
Calories 443

149

November

M	T	W	T	F	S	S	M	T	W	T	F	S	S
14	15	16	17	18	19	20	21	22	23	24	25	26	27

21 Monday

☾ *Last Quarter*

22 Tuesday

23 Wednesday

24 Thursday

25 Friday

M	T	W	T	F	S	S	M	T	W	T	F	S	S
28	29	30	1	2	3	4	5	6	7	8	9	10	11

November
Week 47

Saturday **26**

Sunday **27**
First Sunday in Advent

Bara Pyglyd (Pikelets)

Strong plain flour 450g (1lb)
Salt 1 tsp
Caster sugar 2 tsp
Fast-acting dried yeast 1 tbsp
Milk 600ml (1 pint)
Vegetable oil 1 tbsp
Butter and jam to serve

1 Sift flour into a large bowl. Stir in salt, sugar and yeast. Make a well in centre and pour in milk. Gradually mix in to form a thick batter. Set aside in a warm place for about an hour until batter is frothy and has doubled in size.
2 Lightly brush a 15cm (6in) frying pan with oil and heat until hot. Ladle in sufficient batter to a depth of 2cm (¾in) and cook over a low heat for about 6 minutes until bubbles on surface burst and set. Turn over and cook for a further 2 minutes.
3 Transfer to a wire rack then repeat with remaining batter. Serve warm or cold with butter and jam.

Time 25 mins plus proving	**Makes** 7 **Calories** 279	**Fat** 3.9g of which 1.2g is saturated	V F

151

November

28 Monday

29 Tuesday

● *New Moon*

30 Wednesday

St Andrew's Day

1 Thursday DECEMBER

2 Friday

M	T	W	T	F	S	S	M	T	W	T	F	S	S
5	6	7	8	9	10	11	12	13	14	15	16	17	18

December
Week 48

Saturday 3

Sunday 4

Scotch Woodcock

Eggs 8 (4 whole plus 4 yolks)
Single cream 300ml (½ pint)
Unsalted butter 50g (2oz), softened
White bread 4 slices
Anchovy fillets in olive oil 8, drained
Capers 16, drained
Chopped parsley 2 tbsp

1 Whisk together eggs, egg yolks and cream and season to taste.
2 Melt half the butter in a saucepan and scramble eggs for 4 minutes until softly scrambled.
3 Meanwhile, toast bread on both sides and spread with remaining butter.
4 Pile scrambled egg onto toasts and arrange anchovy fillets in a cross on top of each. Sprinkle with capers and parsley.

Time 10 mins	**Serves** 4	**Fat** 37g of which
	Calories 441	18.9g is saturated

153

December

M	T	W	T	F	S	S	M	T	W	T	F	S	S
28	29	30	1	2	3	4	5	6	7	8	9	10	11

5 Monday

6 Tuesday

7 Wednesday

❯ *First Quarter*

8 Thursday

9 Friday

M	T	W	T	F	S	S	M	T	W	T	F	S	S
12	13	14	15	16	17	18	19	20	21	22	23	24	25

December
Week 49

Saturday **10**

Sunday **11**

Drivers' Fruity Punch

Shloer Red Grape drink
750ml bottle
Cranberry juice 300ml (½ pint)
Cinnamon stick 1, halved
Ground mixed spice ½ tsp
Caster sugar 1 tbsp or to taste
**Cranberry and blood orange
tea** 2 tea bags
Clementine or satsuma
1, peeled and segmented
Cranberries 50g (2oz)

1 Place all ingredients in a saucepan and slowly warm through, stirring, until sugar has dissolved.
2 Bring up to boil, then simmer very gently for 5 minutes, to soften cranberries.
3 Carefully remove tea bags. Pour into heatproof glasses and serve warm.

Time 20 mins   **Serves** 4-6   **Fat** 0.2g of which   [V]
                     Calories 121   0g is saturated

155

December

12 Monday

13 Tuesday

14 Wednesday

○ *Full Moon*

15 Thursday

16 Friday

M	T	W	T	F	S	S	M	T	W	T	F	S	S
19	20	21	22	23	24	25	26	27	28	29	30	31	1

December
Week 50

Saturday **17**

Sunday **18**

Christmas Cupcakes

Muffin cases 12
Cocoa 3 tbsp
Butter 250g (9oz), softened
Caster sugar 175g (6oz)
Eggs 3
Self-raising flour 225g (8oz)
Baking powder 1 tsp
Icing sugar 500g (1lb 2oz)
Full fat soft cheese 200g (7oz)
**Giant chocolate stars and gold
sprinkles with mini stars**
to decorate

1 Preheat oven to
180°C(160°fan)/350°F/Gas 4 and
line a 12 hole muffin tin with
muffin cases.
2 Dissolve cocoa in 3 tbsp hot
water and set aside to cool.
3 Beat together 175g (6oz)
butter, caster sugar, eggs, self-
raising flour and baking powder.
Add cocoa and stir well.
4 Spoon into cases and bake
for 20-25 minutes until well
risen and firm. Leave to cool
for 5 minutes in tin before
transferring to a wire rack.

| **Time** 45 mins | **Makes** 12 | **Fat** 25g of which | V |
| | **Calories** 525 | 15g is saturated | F |

5 Beat together remaining
butter, icing sugar and cheese.
Spoon into a piping bag fitted
with a large star nozzle and pipe
swirls on top. Top with stars and
sprinkles and serve.

December

19 Monday

20 Tuesday

21 Wednesday

(*Last Quarter*
Winter solstice
Winter begins

22 Thursday

23 Friday

M	T	W	T	F	S	S	M	T	W	T	F	S	S
26	27	28	29	30	31	1	2	3	4	5	6	7	8

December
Week 51

Saturday 24

Sunday 25
Christmas Day

Roast Rib of Beef with Thyme & Port

Redcurrant sauce 110g (4oz)
Port 200ml (7fl oz)
Thyme leaves large handful
Lean bone-in rib of beef
2.7kg (6lb)
Garlic bulbs 3, halved
horizontally
Shallots 24, peeled, whole
Plain flour 25g (1oz)
Hot beef stock 600ml (1pint)
**Roast potatoes, stuffing and
sprouts** to serve

1 In a large shallow bowl mix
together redcurrant sauce, port
and thyme.
2 Score beef fat, season, transfer
to bowl with the marinade and
coat well. Cover and chill for
2 hours or overnight.
3 Preheat oven to
180°C(160°fan)/350°F/Gas 4.
Remove meat from bowl
(strain and reserve marinade).
Place on a rack in a roasting tin
and open roast for preferred
time (see p25). After 30 minutes
cover with foil.

Time 3 hrs	Serves 8-10	Fat 18g of which
plus marinating	Calories 476	7.9g is saturated

4 45 minutes before end of
cooking time, remove rack from
tin, add garlic and shallots
and place joint directly on top.
Return to oven.

5 Make gravy using juices in tin,
flour, stock and 150ml (¼ pint)
of marinade. Simmer for 8-10
minutes. Strain, then serve with
beef and accompaniments.

December

26 Monday

Boxing Day
Bank Holiday, UK

27 Tuesday

Bank Holiday, UK

28 Wednesday

29 Thursday

● *New Moon*

30 Friday

M	T	W	T	F	S	S	M	T	W	T	F	S	S
2	3	4	5	6	7	8	9	10	11	12	13	14	15

December
Week 52

Saturday **31**
New Year's Eve

JANUARY 2017 Sunday **1**
New Year's Day

White Chocolate Cheesecake

Butter 75g (3oz), melted
Ginger nuts 200g (7oz), crushed
Good quality white chocolate 350g (12oz), chopped, plus extra, shaved, to decorate
Double cream 150ml (¼ pint)
Full fat cream cheese 500g (1lb 2oz)
Frozen cranberries 150g (5oz)
Caster sugar 125g (4½oz)
Orange juice 125ml (4fl oz)

1 Mix together butter and biscuits. Press into the base of a 20.5cm (8in) round loose-based tin. Chill for 10 minutes to firm.
2 Place chocolate in a heatproof bowl. In a saucepan heat cream until almost simmering then pour over chocolate. Stir well until chocolate has melted then leave to cool.
3 Beat cheese until soft. Fold into chocolate cream and mix well. Spoon over biscuit base and smooth the surface. Cover with cling film and chill for 8 hours, or preferably overnight, until set.

Time 45 mins plus chilling	**Serves** 8-10 **Calories** 678	**Fat** 51g of which 31.4g is saturated

4 Place cranberries, sugar and juice in a saucepan and heat gently, stirring, until sugar has dissolved. Bring slowly up to boil, then simmer for 5-10 minutes.

5 Reserve 12, then blend rest of cranberries until smooth. Unmould cheesecake. Decorate with chocolate and cranberries and serve with cranberry coulis.

161

Notes

Notes

Notes

Notes

Have you ordered next year's Dairy Diary?

Three ways to order:

FROM YOUR MILKMAN
Use the **order form on p170**, or, if you usually order via your dairy's website, order online.

TELEPHONE
If you do not have a milkman, ring **0845 0948 128** (calls charged at local rate) or **01425 463390** (if calling from a mobile). Place your order over the phone and your diary will be posted to you.

ONLINE
Visit **dairydiary.co.uk**
See full details of the 2017 Dairy Diary and other products.

Reserve YOUR COPY OF THE DAIRY DIARY 2017

To order your copy of the 2017 Dairy Diary, please fill in the order form overleaf and leave it out for your milkman with your empties from September 2016.

If you usually order via your dairy's website, order online.

Dairy Diary 2017

Order FORM

MILKMAN PLEASE LEAVE ME:

☐ copies of the
2017 Dairy Diary

☐ copies of the 2017
Dairy Diary Set

Name ....

Address..

....

....

....

....

Postcode..

Thank you
Leave out for your milkman from September 2016
onwards

Recipe INDEX

Roast Beef Hash with Eggs   **71**
(f:3g, su:0g, sa:0.5g)

Roast Rib of Beef with Thyme & Port   **159**
(f:1g, su:0g, sa:1.3g)

Salmon with Roast Red Pepper Salad   **125**
(f:1.8g, su:0g, sa:0.8g)

Spicy Sausage & Tomato Pasta   **97**
(f:7.5g, su:0g, sa:3.2g)

Sticky Lamb Ribs   **89**
(f:0.4g, su:12g, sa:1.5g)

Sweet Chilli Stir-Fried Pork   **59**
(f:3.8g, su:1.2g, sa:1.2g)

SIDE DISHES & SAUCES

Parmigiano Reggiano Herby Potato Wedges   **115**
(f:2.1g, su:0g, sa:0.4g)

Spicy Lime Courgettes   **119**
(f:0.6g, su:5g, sa:0g)

Turmeric Pickled Cauliflower   **73**
(f:0.8g, su:4g, sa:0g)

DESSERTS

Chocolate Cookie Sandwiches   **75**
(f:0.8g, su:8g, sa:0.2g)

Hot Cross Bun & Butter Pudding   **83**
(f:1.3g, su:25g, sa:0.5g)

Irish Cream Chocolate Trifles   **79**
(f:0.7g, su:27g, sa:0.3g)

Napoleons   **33**
(f:0.4g, su:55g, sa:0.8g)

Pear & Ginger Sorbet   **131**
(f:2.2g, su:25g, sa:0g)

Raspberry Roulade   **31**
(f:2g, su:33g, sa:0.1g)

Scotch Pancakes with Rhubarb Compote   **69**
(f:3.2g, su:20g, sa:0.4g)

Strawberry Jellies   **99**
(f:1.5g, su:9g, sa:0g)

White Chocolate Cheesecake   **161**
(f:0.6g, su:42g, sa:0.8g)

RECIPE NOTES

Nutritional information has been calculated by portion or item. Where there are portion variations, e.g. serves 6-8, the analysis given is based on the larger number. Calories, fat and saturated fat is provided on the recipe page, fibre, sugar and salt is given in the recipe index.

V Suitable for vegetarians, provided an appropriate cheese or yogurt is used.

F Suitable for freezing.

Recipes using nuts or nut products are not suitable for young children or those with a nut allergy.

Certain at-risk groups, such as pregnant women, babies and sick or elderly people should not eat raw or lightly cooked eggs.

CAKES & BAKES

Bara Pyglyd (Pikelets)   **151**
(f:2.7g, su:1g, sa:0.8g)

Chorizo & Cheddar Scones   **147**
(f:0.9g, su:0g, sa:0.4g)

Christmas Cupcakes   **157**
(f:1g, su:16g, sa:0.8g)

Coconut Raspberry Friands   **127**
(f:2.4g, su:19g, sa:0.3g)

Cornish Fairings   **123**
(f:0.3g, su:6g, sa:0.4g)

Easter Egg Cake Pops   **81**
(f:0.6g, su:23g, sa:0.3g)

Homebaked Sally Lunns   **107**
(f:5.3g, su:0g, sa:2g)

Maids of Honour   **101**
(f:0.6g, su:5.5g, sa:0.2g)

Westmorland Pepper Cake   **65**
(f:1.1g, su:14g, sa:0.3g)

MISCELLANEOUS

Blueberry Bircher Muesli   **109**
(f:8.2g, su:9.3g, sa:0.2g)

Drivers' Fruity Punch   **155**
(f:0.2g, su:21g, sa:0g)

Peanut Butter Hot Chocolate   **145**
(f:0.2g, su:9.9g, sa:0.4g)

Trick or Treat Toffee Apples   **143**
(f:1.6g, su:35g, sa:0.1g)

Note: Abbreviations f: fibre; su: sugar, and sa; salt per portion.

Year planner 2017

JANUARY		FEBRUARY	MARCH	
1 **Sun**		1 Wed	1 Wed	
2 Mon	BANK HOLIDAY	2 Thu	2 Thu	
3 Tue	BANK HOLIDAY SCOTLAND	3 Fri	3 Fri	
4 Wed		4 **Sat**	4 **Sat**	
5 Thu		5 **Sun**	5 **Sun**	
6 Fri		6 Mon	6 Mon	
7 **Sat**		7 Tue	7 Tue	
8 **Sun**		8 Wed	8 Wed	
9 Mon		9 Thu	9 Thu	
10 Tue		10 Fri	10 Fri	
11 Wed		11 **Sat**	11 **Sat**	
12 Thu		12 **Sun**	12 **Sun**	
13 Fri		13 Mon	13 Mon	
14 **Sat**		14 Tue	14 Tue	
15 **Sun**		15 Wed	15 Wed	
16 Mon		16 Thu	16 Thu	
17 Tue		17 Fri	17 Fri	BANK HOLIDAY N IRELAND
18 Wed		18 **Sat**	18 **Sat**	
19 Thu		19 **Sun**	19 **Sun**	
20 Fri		20 Mon	20 Mon	
21 **Sat**		21 Tue	21 Tue	
22 **Sun**		22 Wed	22 Wed	
23 Mon		23 Thu	23 Thu	
24 Tue		24 Fri	24 Fri	
25 Wed		25 **Sat**	25 **Sat**	
26 Thu		26 **Sun**	26 **Sun**	
27 Fri		27 Mon	27 Mon	
28 **Sat**		28 Tue	28 Tue	
29 **Sun**			29 Wed	
30 Mon			30 Thu	
31 Tue			31 Fri	

APRIL		MAY		JUNE	
1	Sat	1	Mon BANK HOLIDAY	1	Thu
2	Sun	2	Tue	2	Fri
3	Mon	3	Wed	3	Sat
4	Tue	4	Thu	4	Sun
5	Wed	5	Fri	5	Mon
6	Thu	6	Sat	6	Tue
7	Fri	7	Sun	7	Wed
8	Sat	8	Mon	8	Thu
9	Sun	9	Tue	9	Fri
10	Mon	10	Wed	10	Sat
11	Tue	11	Thu	11	Sun
12	Wed	12	Fri	12	Mon
13	Thu	13	Sat	13	Tue
14	Fri BANK HOLIDAY	14	Sun	14	Wed
15	Sat	15	Mon	15	Thu
16	Sun	16	Tue	16	Fri
17	Mon BANK HOLIDAY	17	Wed	17	Sat
18	Tue	18	Thu	18	Sun
19	Wed	19	Fri	19	Mon
20	Thu	20	Sat	20	Tue
21	Fri	21	Sun	21	Wed
22	Sat	22	Mon	22	Thu
23	Sun	23	Tue	23	Fri
24	Mon	24	Wed	24	Sat
25	Tue	25	Thu	25	Sun
26	Wed	26	Fri	26	Mon
27	Thu	27	Sat	27	Tue
28	Fri	28	Sun	28	Wed
29	Sat	29	Mon BANK HOLIDAY	29	Thu
30	Sun	30	Tue	30	Fri
		31	Wed		

P.T.O. July–December 2017

Year planner 2017

JULY		AUGUST		SEPTEMBER	
1	Sat	1	Tue	1	Fri
2	Sun	2	Wed	2	Sat
3	Mon	3	Thu	3	Sun
4	Tue	4	Fri	4	Mon
5	Wed	5	Sat	5	Tue
6	Thu	6	Sun	6	Wed
7	Fri	7	Mon BANK HOLIDAY SCOTLAND	7	Thu
8	Sat	8	Tue	8	Fri
9	Sun	9	Wed	9	Sat
10	Mon	10	Thu	10	Sun
11	Tue	11	Fri	11	Mon
12	Wed BANK HOLIDAY N IRELAND	12	Sat	12	Tue
13	Thu	13	Sun	13	Wed
14	Fri	14	Mon	14	Thu
15	Sat	15	Tue	15	Fri
16	Sun	16	Wed	16	Sat
17	Mon	17	Thu	17	Sun
18	Tue	18	Fri	18	Mon
19	Wed	19	Sat	19	Tue
20	Thu	20	Sun	20	Wed
21	Fri	21	Mon	21	Thu
22	Sat	22	Tue	22	Fri
23	Sun	23	Wed	23	Sat
24	Mon	24	Thu	24	Sun
25	Tue	25	Fri	25	Mon
26	Wed	26	Sat	26	Tue
27	Thu	27	Sun	27	Wed
28	Fri	28	Mon BANK HOLIDAY	28	Thu
29	Sat	29	Tue	29	Fri
30	Sun	30	Wed	30	Sat
31	Mon	31	Thu		

OCTOBER	NOVEMBER	DECEMBER
1 Sun	1 Wed	1 Fri
2 Mon	2 Thu	2 Sat
3 Tue	3 Fri	3 Sun
4 Wed	4 Sat	4 Mon
5 Thu	5 Sun	5 Tue
6 Fri	6 Mon	6 Wed
7 Sat	7 Tue	7 Thu
8 Sun	8 Wed	8 Fri
9 Mon	9 Thu	9 Sat
10 Tue	10 Fri	10 Sun
11 Wed	11 Sat	11 Mon
12 Thu	12 Sun	12 Tue
13 Fri	13 Mon	13 Wed
14 Sat	14 Tue	14 Thu
15 Sun	15 Wed	15 Fri
16 Mon	16 Thu	16 Sat
17 Tue	17 Fri	17 Sun
18 Wed	18 Sat	18 Mon
19 Thu	19 Sun	19 Tue
20 Fri	20 Mon	20 Wed
21 Sat	21 Tue	21 Thu
22 Sun	22 Wed	22 Fri
23 Mon	23 Thu	23 Sat
24 Tue	24 Fri	24 Sun
25 Wed	25 Sat	25 Mon BANK HOLIDAY
26 Thu	26 Sun	26 Tue BANK HOLIDAY
27 Fri	27 Mon	27 Wed
28 Sat	28 Tue	28 Thu
29 Sun	29 Wed	29 Fri
30 Mon	30 Thu	30 Sat
31 Tue		31 Sun

Acknowledgements

Executive Editor
Nick Rowe
Managing Editor
Emily Davenport

Editor
Marion Paull
Art Editor
Karen Perry

Front Cover Image
GAP Photos/Friedrich Strauss
Production
Cath Linter

Photographer Steve Lee
Food Stylist Sara Lewis
Props Stylist Jo Harris
Recipe Writer Lucy Knox
Recipe Testing Richard Davenport
Claire Nadin
Lucy Padget
Chris Perry
Laura Pickering
Gudrun Waskett

Nutritional analysis
Paul McArdle

Special thanks Kate Bailey
Aune Butt
Graham Meigh
Penny Meigh
Julia Robinson
Denise
Spencer-Walker

The Dairy Diary is delivered directly to your door by your local milkman
Eaglemoss Consumer Publications Ltd
Electra House, Electra Way, Crewe Business Park, Crewe, Cheshire CW1 6GL
Telephone: 01270 270050
Dairy Diary Orders Telephone: 0845 0948 128
Website: dairydiary.co.uk
Blog: dairydiarychat.co.uk